WOMAN'S OWN

Book of

HOUSE PLANTS

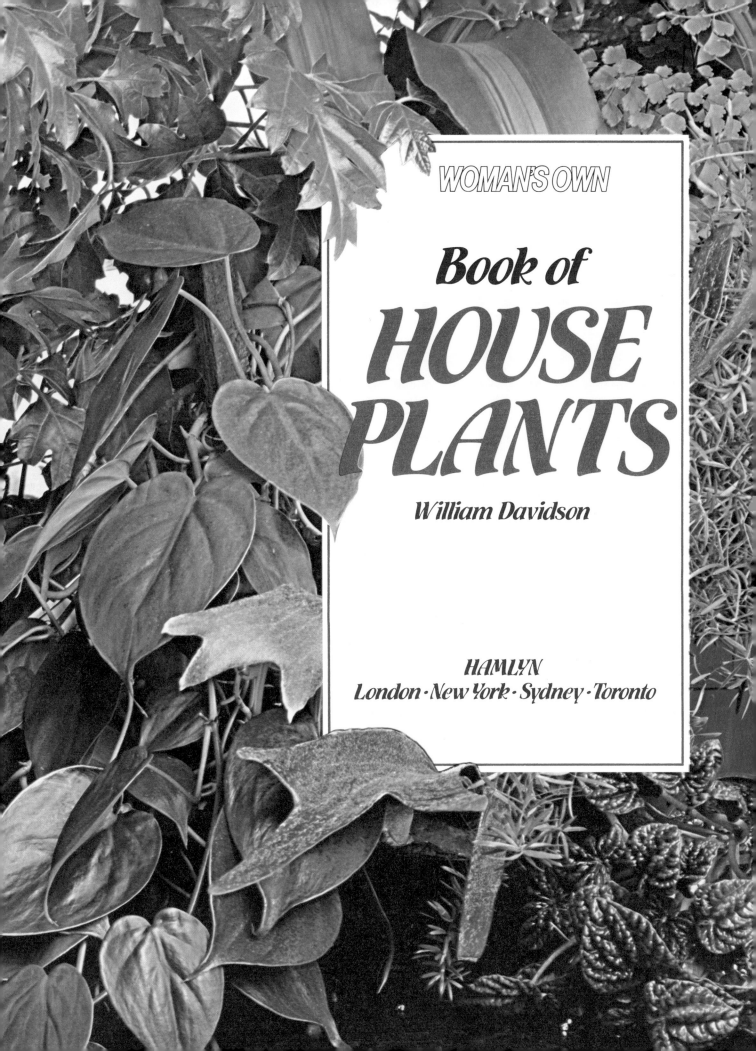

WOMAN'S OWN

Book of
HOUSE
PLANTS

William Davidson

HAMLYN
London · New York · Sydney · Toronto

ACKNOWLEDGEMENTS

The editor would like to thank Mr and Mrs L. Liebster for
allowing us to take photographs of houseplants in their home and
Carol Bowen for lending Bryony

Colour photographs by: **Pat Brindley** (p 15, p 18, p 51 *top*, p 106,
p 126 and p 134 *bottom*); **Harry Smith Horticultural Photographic
Collection** (p 19 *top and bottom right*, p 22, p 42, p 74, p 82, p 83,
p 122, p 127 *top* and p 135); **Peter Stiles** (p 127 *bottom right*); **Michael
Warren** (p 14 *top*, p 55, p 75 *top*, p 107 *bottom* and p 119) and
Paul Williams (endpaper, title page, introduction, p 23, pp 46–47,
p 50, p 54, pp 78–9, p 86, pp 110–111, p 114, p 123 and pp 130–131).

First published in 1969
revised edition published in 1980 by
The Hamlyn Publishing Group Limited
London · New York · Sydney · Toronto
Astronaut House, Feltham, Middlesex

Filmset in England by Tradespools Limited, Frome, Somerset in
10 on 11 pt. Apollo
Printed in Singapore

CONTENTS

*T*he popularity of houseplants has now reached such proportions that it is unusual to visit a house in which no plant at all is grown. One can confidently predict that this current enthusiasm will continue for many years, especially as the proportions of modern living rooms with their often rather severe outlines and large windows are particularly well suited to a plant display of some kind. Once bitten by the bug of houseplant growing, the tendency seems to be to utilise every possible corner of the house – so beware!

This book is designed for those who want to know something about the culture of plants indoors without necessarily delving too deeply into their background and nomenclature. For information I have drawn on over 20 years of experience of growing, exhibiting, talking, advising – in fact, almost 'living' houseplants. And, above all, I have kept in mind the endless stream of questions that have been asked over the years.

Though I have not knowingly sought information from the book of any other author, I feel sure that many of my acquaintances will, however, recognise some of my material as their personal opinions. For this I apologise, if apology is necessary.

I am often asked the simple question, 'What actually is a houseplant?' The answer is equally simple: 'Any plant that forms a permanent part of room decoration'. So, my Granny, in the far north of Scotland, will be pleased to know that her 'shamrock' (oxalis), humble though it is, can lay claim to being a houseplant.

Perhaps I should point out that I have not set out to give brief information on the largest possible number of plants but have endeavoured to discuss fewer plants more fully, and provide more general advice on plant culture indoors. Well-grown houseplants, attractively displayed, can add greatly to the pleasures of the home.

CHAPTER 1
Selection and display

Eventual success with houseplants depends very often on the quality of plant initially purchased. Average indoor conditions, on the whole, leave much to be desired when seeking the ideal environment in which to grow plants of any kind. Consequently it stands to reason that a plant of inferior quality, when introduced to room conditions, will quickly deteriorate, whereas the robust plant with a vigorous, healthy root system, and free from pests, will have a much better chance of survival.

Sales outlets

Where once the sale of potted plants was the prerogative of the florist or the nurserymen, we now see them retailed in all sorts of unlikely places such as supermarkets and department stores, where they seem to vie with dresses and shoes as potential purchases for anyone having cash available. Although these surroundings may not at first sight appear very appropriate for such things as Swiss cheese plants and creeping figs, most store managers have learned a lot as the business expanded and many care for their plants extremely well. However, one must still exercise a little care when making a selection – the most important requirement would seem to be that the plants themselves should have a cared for look. Some retailers treat the plants in much the same way as the other merchandise placing the plants in dark corners or draughts, and forgetting that they must be watered. Look over the plant's display area before deciding to purchase. Plants must have a suitable place while they are in the store, and they must also have essential attention in respect of watering, even feeding. With a little care, plants in a well-lit, well-heated and ventilated store can do infinitely better than the same plants placed in a flower shop, for example, that may lack these modern facilities.

You will find good and bad in all houseplant sales outlets, therefore a watchful eye must be kept when purchasing them. If you are a beginner then it is a good idea to take someone along who knows something about it and let them decide until you acquire a bit of skill in detecting good from bad.

Amongst my colleagues I hear a lot of criticism about the way some department stores handle houseplants but, to my mind, rather than harm the houseplant trade it simply puts plants within the reach of many people who would otherwise not have bothered to buy them. Some people who fight shy of entering a flower shop or visiting a garden centre will happily pick up a plant while attending to the family shopping. I can see no objection to purchasing healthy plants from competent staff in premises that are in most instances splendidly suited to the care of houseplants.

More and more garden centres are also cropping up, and needless to say more and more of them are selling indoor plants – some doing a fine job of caring for them while others do not seem to have the first idea of where they should begin. For my sins, I run quarterly training courses at the nursery for people in our trade in an effort to educate them in the needs of plants, and these have without doubt been successful in improving standards at many establishments. Alas, they appear to have little effect on the very busy people in some areas of our trade – they still manage to forget watering, feeding, pest control, shading the glass, and numerous other essential needs of potted plants while they are in transit from the grower to the eventual purchaser.

A simple arrangement of houseplants is often the most effective

Far left, top An old copper kettle makes an unusual container for a small Fittonia argyroneura

Far left, bottom An occasional table is used to give a fatshedera plant a prominent position. The upright shape of this plant is contrasted with the spreading leaves of the *Platycerium alcicorne*

Left A garden trug is an attractive container for a selection of flowering and foliage plants. An arrangement of this type can be changed around as frequently as desired

Choosing a good quality plant

Regardless of the supplier, it still applies that one must have an eye for a plant and one should never forget that the quality of the purchased plant can make all the difference to its eventual performance indoors. Check the plant over when purchasing, and do make a thorough check of the foliage should there be any suspicion of pests being present; there is no point in introducing unwanted visitors that may well in time damage other plants in one's collection. There are, however, other ways of detecting good from bad; and one of the most important points is to ensure that plants are actively growing, and not stunted or limp at the tips. Even in winter, greenhouse-grown pot plants should make a reasonable amount of growth, though there are a few exceptions, such as the rubber plant (*Ficus elastica robusta*).

If a plant has a fresh, crisp appearance this is another point in favour of purchase. Staked plants should look as if the growth is actually climbing the stake, and one ought to avoid plants that are hanging limply around their support. Hard-baked or thoroughly saturated composts are both signs of mismanagement on the part of the supplier, and are two more reasons for directing your purse and your footsteps to the next shop along the road.

Well-furnished plants

The professional grower is always impressed on seeing what he terms 'a well-furnished plant'. By this he means a plant of full appearance with leaves all the way down the stem; and, given the choice, he would invariably select the smaller, well-furnished plant in preference to the tall, leggy one. Production of such a plant takes more time and requires frequent pinching of leading shoots to encourage a bushy appearance, so one should expect to pay a little more for it. Missing, yellow, or damaged leaves are further indications of indifferent culture and handling.

Defects to look for in flowering plants

With flowering pot plants it is also important to look for the same defects that one might expect to find in foliage plants: yellow and missing leaves, an untidy appearance and so on. Equally, or perhaps more important, is the need to buy plants that are not 'blown' or in full flower, though it is also important that flowering plants should not be too backward when purchased. The aim should be to select plants with a reasonable amount of colour showing and plenty of young buds still to open that will give you pleasure in the months to come. There are exceptions, though; the pleasure of seeing a friend's face light up on being presented with something as exciting as an *Azalea indica* in full bloom can make the lasting qualities of the plant seem unimportant.

Always try to buy a well-furnished plant with leaves well down the stem or a bushy appearance

Plastic pots

Much controversy still reigns over the pros and cons of plastic pots compared to clay ones. A few years ago I would have unhesitatingly selected the plant growing in a clay pot in preference to an equally good, often better plant growing in a plastic pot. Nor does it seem so long ago that the rather conservative race of people generally referred to as gardeners, or growers, were shaking their heads disapprovingly at the thought of growing difficult or temperamental plants such as hydrangeas, cyclamen or poinsettias in plastic pots. However, as we all know, these plants are now almost all grown in the lighter pot, and it would seem that the clay pot with its many drawbacks is dying a comparatively rapid death. Have no qualms about selecting the plastic pot; most plants do equally well in them and many do very much better.

A slight change in growing technique is necessary for plants in plastic pots, in that they require very much less water than similar plants growing in clay pots. Some years ago a meticulously controlled experiment was carried out with clay and plastic pots in order to estimate the growth difference of plants grown in identical conditions. It was found that the different pots had very little effect on the plants. Where a mixed batch of pots was watered according to the requirements of the clay pots, the plastic ones became much too wet, and when the treatment was reversed, the compost in the clay pots became much too dry. In every other respect the clean, light and easily handled plastic pot gave a very good account of itself.

When growing African violets (saintpaulias), the plastic pot has a marked advantage over the clay, as the latter absorbs moisture that will quickly rot through any leafstalks that may rest on the rim of the pot. An aluminium foil, or silver paper protective cover, kneaded around the edge of the clay pot is essential in order to prevent leafstalks becoming wet.

Taking your plants home

Purchasing a suitable plant is one thing, but taking it from the shop to the home unprotected can often undo all the good work of the nurseryman. So when acquiring plants during the colder months insist on adequate wrapping. When making your choice, do not pass over the clean plant that has been carefully wrapped. Plants, as a rule, are reared in warm greenhouses and, though they quickly adapt themselves to cooler indoor conditions, a short

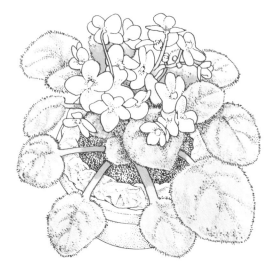

Knead aluminium foil round the edge of a clay pot to prevent the stalks of African violet leaves taking up moisture and rotting

spell in below freezing conditions will often prove fatal. The damage may not be apparent until some time later.

Mention of cold conditions suggests a further precaution when making one's purchase. Generally speaking, there are few shops where space is not a permanent problem, and this is frequently made obvious by the number of plants standing outside on the pavement. This may be all very well for the hardier type of indoor plant during the summer months, but the sight of a *Begonia rex* propped against the outside wall of a shop in the middle of March is enough to chill the blood. Need one be warned not to buy from the box outside, or from the inconsiderate person who placed it there?

Is it difficult to grow?

Of the various houseplants available, the majority are comparatively easy to manage and with reasonable care will give several years pleasure, while others are more trying and will test the skill of the most competent houseplant grower. Several nurserymen are wise enough to attach labels to their products with clearly printed advice regarding each particular plant, and stating whether they are easy or difficult to manage indoors. When purchasing plants needing higher temperatures, like codiaeums (crotons) and dieffenbachias, it should be realised that these are expendable but will give great pleasure, if only for a few months in some cases. Keen plantsmen, however, seem to manage many of them very well once the plants have settled down in their new environments. It should not be forgotten that when compared with an expensive bunch of flowers, the exotic foliage plant is indeed good value for money.

The conventional carboy is just one type of container that can be used to create a miniature garden with a controlled environment
Far left A sweet jar, an unheated propagating tray and a glass have all been used for this purpose
Left The traditional Wardian case invented by Dr Ward for delicate plants
Bottom left Although a complete contrast in appearance this modern 'bubble' terrarium performs much the same function as the Wardian case
Bottom right An old fish tank has been used to create a moist environment for small ferns

Displaying houseplants

Good display of house plants can make all the difference to their effectiveness as an ornamental feature in the home. And one of the best ways of achieving this is to group the plants in some sort of container, either sinking the pots into damp peat or removing the plants from their pots and setting them in compost. When a planting-up of this kind is attempted it is important to use slow-growing plants with similar cultural requirements and not to use too many – they must have space to expand.

To be really effective choose plants with different heights, leaf shapes and colours but keep the height in proportion to the depth of the container.

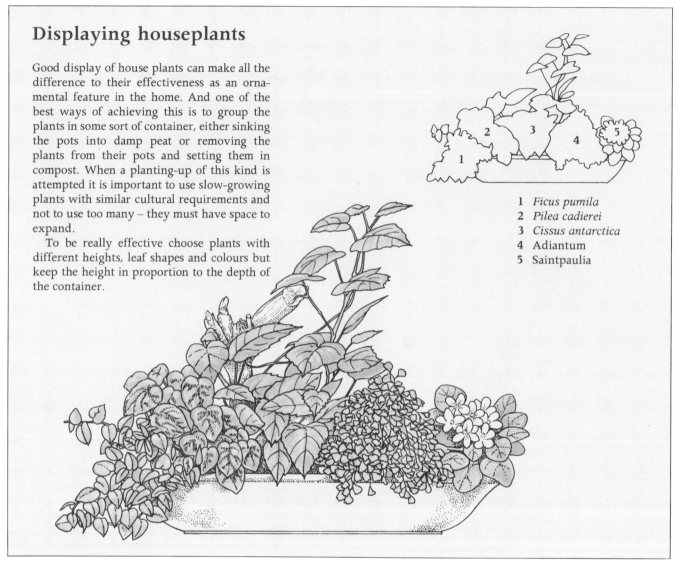

1 *Ficus pumila*
2 *Pilea cadierei*
3 *Cissus antarctica*
4 *Adiantum*
5 *Saintpaulia*

Containers & display

Suitable containers of adequate size are one of the most important aids to plant display, be it a piece of ornamental pottery for a single pot, or an elaborate container for a group of plants. When purchasing an outer decorative pot for a plant already in your possession take the simple precaution of either measuring the plant's pot before setting out on your errand, or, better still, take an empty pot with you of similar size to the one in which your plant is growing. Where possible, containers should be slightly larger than the pot in order that a layer of moist pebbles can be placed in the bottom of the decorative pot for your plant to stand on.

When selecting or making display containers, keep in mind the thought that the height of plants is almost invariably governed by the dimensions of the pot in which the plant is growing. The following approximate guide to relative sizes may be helpful: a $3\frac{1}{2}$-in diameter pot for a plant about 15 in to 18 in tall; 5-in pot for a plant about 20 in to 26 in tall; a 7-in ($3\frac{1}{2}$ ft to $4\frac{1}{2}$ ft) tall; and a 9-in pot for a plant about 5 ft to 7 ft tall. Plants in larger pots should always be seen before finalising purchase; otherwise, you may, for example, purchase a 4 ft tall monstera plant only to find that the spread of the plant is much too large for the position earmarked for it.

The use of larger containers accommodating a number of plants poses the question of whether one should employ the free-planting method, or simply plunge plant pots to their rims in moist peat. If the first method is adopted the container should be almost filled with compost and the plants placed on the compost in suitable positions to simplify the actual planting operation which follows. I would suggest that one or two spaces are left for flowering plants; do this by inserting an empty pot or two into the compost. These can be easily removed and replaced with a flowering plant at almost any time. When the plants are freely planted, growth will be much more vigorous, but there will be less opportunity for rearranging them.

If plants are left in their pots, probably the best plunging medium is moist peat, as plants are easily arranged in this and can be tilted at just the right angle for the finished effect. If the dark peat is found to be objectionable, a scattering of gravel on the surface of the peat will improve the appearance. Where plants with differing water requirements are free-planted in the same container it is wise to strike a happy medium when watering, and, if anything, one should err on the side of dryness rather than making the soil over-moist.

One should not be afraid of getting one's hands dirty occasionally when working with plants, even if it is only to prod a finger into the soil to test its water requirements. Nevertheless, it would be regrettable if a potential houseplant owner were to be put off by my references to soil, peat and the like. Take heart, there are many other ways of displaying plants, and inspection of the wide variety of plant stands and containers available in almost any good department store or florist's shop will provide ample inspiration. If space is limited, the standard type of plant trough can be used to get the maximum number of plants into the minimum amount of space. However, a well-arranged plant table always appeals to me as providing a clean and effective display that is easily maintained.

Plants in rooms

We have a lot to learn about plant display in a large living room of around 20 ft by 10 ft and our continental neighbours provide us with good examples.

Taking a typical block of flats (where indoor plants mean so much to those without gardens) almost anywhere in the country as a yard-stick, I am afraid that the way houseplants are displayed compares most unfavourably with similar homes on the other side of the North Sea. Recently I had the pleasure of spending a holiday in Amstelveen, a suburb of Amsterdam, where I lived in a box-shaped room, with a large plate glass window, in a box-shaped block of flats. During the day these flats had little to commend them, other than immaculately tended gardens, compared to similar developments here. However, during darkness, when the room lights were switched

on, the place became a fascinating fairyland for me. My wife and I walked around and unashamedly stared into many of the delightful rooms with their diffused lights and remarkable range of superbly grown houseplants. I got the feeling that our Dutch hosts derived a certain amount of pleasure when someone stopped and paid them the compliment of admiring their contribution to the general charm of the neighbourhood. Need one add that a tour of a similar area here would be a pretty dismal business – and it could all so easily be changed, with a little effort.

Ingredients for success

Doubtless the bare minimum of curtain draped around the windows of Dutch homes during the day is one reason for them being able to grow plants of infinitely better quality than most of us here. I include myself, as I have been fighting a losing battle with my wife over the years to have windows freed from light obstruction. Alas, privacy is still more important. Of all the considerations when arranging plants indoors, perhaps the most important is to ensure that they have a light position in which to grow.

A further possible reason for our continental neighbours' success with plants is that they always seem to have plenty; seldom less than twenty in the average living room. There seems little doubt that plants do better when grouped together, be they in the greenhouse or the home, and the single plant with a room to itself rarely prospers. Like ourselves, plants seem to need company, and soon deteriorate in solitary confinement.

The continental grower is more fortunate than his British counterpart in that there are many more occasions, other than the usual ones, for the giving of flowers and plants as gifts. Birthdays and Christmas are important present-giving times, but it is also quite common for the continental housewife to find a welcoming array of plants and flowers awaiting her on return from her annual summer holiday. Plants play such an important part in room decoration that it is not uncommon to find specially designed plant windows in many homes; these are positioned where plants will not be exposed to strong midday sun. Such windows have special tiled sills, which are deeper than usual and are often provided with suitable drainage, so that there is no concern when water is spilt.

An extension of this idea is the plant room, where the bare minimum of furniture is used and plants are given pride of place. These rooms are not unlike the Victorian conservatory, except for the fact that they are integral

continued on page 24

The *Kitchen*

Kitchens are usually very good places in which to grow houseplants. Conditions of warmth, humidity and light are all beneficial to the great majority of plants. However in many kitchens the temperature falls dramatically at night, particularly in the winter, so avoid plants which need a consistently high temperature. A variegated rubber plant in an old casserole dish looks fitting in kitchen surroundings **(below)**. A small fern and *Scindapsus aureus* complete the arrangement. Various plants have been carefully arranged in a family kitchen to make it look attractive without interfering with the cooking and eating **(right)**. Notice especially the trailing *Scindapsus aureus* on the right of the picture, grown on the hydroponic system, the small cacti on the windowsill and the pretty hanging basket which, of course, takes up no valuable surface space.

parts of the house with large plate glass windows, carpeted floors and other such comforts.

Plants as a special feature

In 1978 I was given sole charge of designing and arranging Rochford's Chelsea Flower Show display. The design was simple, the plants of superb quality, and everything went right on the day. The exhibit was awarded a Gold Medal at the show, and later in the year it was awarded the much coveted Lawrence Medal for the best exhibit shown to the Society during the course of the entire year.

The design was simple and all the plants were arranged so that they appeared in what I thought could well have been a natural setting. All too often one sees plant arrangements where the plants are put in hopelessly unnatural settings. The first lesson to be learned is that plants must never be overcrowded, and should not be fitted into an impossible location simply because it is pretty, or whatever.

Climbing plants Recently I was asked to recommend plants for placing either side of an arched opening between two rooms. The suggestion was that a single plant in an attractive container should be placed on either side and that the plants should be soft and flexible rather than rigid, the idea being that they would grow up and be trained around the archway eventually creating a green arbour effect. In the end the chosen plant was the weeping fig, *Ficus benjamina*; two were placed at either side of the entrance. As this plant gets older the stems become less flexible, but in the early stages they can be tied in to provide a very pleasing weeping effect.

More of a clinging plant, but equally useful in providing cover for a wall as a climbing plant is grape ivy, *Rhoicissus rhomboidea*; there is also the newer version with serrated leaves, *Rhoicissus ellendanica*. If a more rampant green-foliaged climber is wanted then there can be no better choice than *Tetrastigma voinierianum*, but it is not the plant for the limited space of a small room.

Hallways For a wide step, or for the more spacious entrance hall there are some fine plants that can be placed as individual attractions. Best known of these is probably the Swiss cheese plant, *Monstera deliciosa*, with its attractive serrated green leaves and bushy though reasonably compact habit of growth. Of a duller shade of green with fans of oval-shaped fingered leaves attached to stout petioles *Schefflera digitata* is a splendid upright plant. With both of these some of the lower leaves will almost inevitably be lost in time;

Monstera deliciosa or Swiss cheese plant is ideal for a light, spacious, draught-proof hallway

this is natural in most plants as they age. To help refurbish the lower and denuded portion of the stem, it is a good idea to introduce a small new plant at the base when the larger one is being potted on. For similar locations, particularly in cooler temperatures, one could consider *Aralia sieboldii* (syn. *Fatsia japonica*), which is reminiscent of the Swiss cheese plant.

A fireplace display During the summer months the disused fireplace is a favourite position for indoor plants. When such a position is chosen for plants, take the precaution of blocking off the chimney vent with a piece of cardboard, otherwise they will quickly succumb to the draughty conditions. Unless the room is particularly well lit it is better to confine one's choice to the hardier varieties when decorating the fireplace, preferably to the green-leaved sorts. The fireplace is often the ideal place for arranging a temporary display of plants for a special occasion, when other space may be at a premium.

A group of small plants

Should a solitary plant be considered inadequate then one can go in for a collection in a larger container. Make sure that the plants you choose are compatible with regard to soil and atmospheric requirements, and mix leaf shapes and colour as well as size when forming the group. Water-grown plants, that survive very well with no soil whatsoever around their roots, could well be the ideal answer for a mixed grouping.

Small, individual plants are not so easily managed if they are to form an effective display, and for maximum effect it is often better to place such plants in a glass case of some kind – an old fish tank (even a new one!) being most suitable. The plants will grow extremely well as they are shielded from draughts and can create their own microclimate. Such containers seem to me to be much more satisfactory than more conventional bottle gardens that always appear overcrowded and are difficult to get into to perform essential chores.

As I do my rounds I see an ever-increasing number of small greenhouses that are well suited for indoor use and the care of more tender houseplants. Plants in these are immediately accessible, and at minimal cost one can provide the temperature that the plants require without the cost of heating the entire room. Even a single light bulb will offer a surprisingly pleasant amount of warmth in a closed, glassed area indoors, and the additional light will also improve the performance of the plants as well as enhancing them visually. Small marantas, fittonias and selaginellas are fine for enclosed cases, as are African violets (saintpaulias) and smaller ferns.

Plants for dark corners

Time and time again I have been asked for advice on the most suitable plant for a dark corner. My reaction is to suggest the dear old cast iron plant (aspidistra) which will tolerate the most trying conditions without batting an eyelid, or, should we say, shedding a leaf.

For the slightly less dark areas of a room there are some fine plants to choose from, and one of the finest is the old favourite, the nephrolepis fern. These ferns are available in many splendid varieties, and have large fronds of greenery that will radiate from the pot in all directions. Keep them moist, sprayed over and in the shade and they will give endless pleasure as pedestal subjects.

Philodendron scandens and *Rhoicissus rhomboidea* are also fine trailing plants for shady corners. A plant that has been giving me considerable pleasure and very little bother in recent years is *Scindapsus aureus*. It is especially useful for providing contrast in areas of solid green leaf on account of its very attractive golden-yellow variegation.

In lighter and cooler locations the ivies will do well, and an old indestructible (surviving in almost any location) is the spider plant (*Chlorophytum comosum*). This is particularly attractive as a hanging plant when the young plantlets begin to spread in all directions thrown out on long stalks from the parent. For the more ambitious, though not such a difficult plant in my experience, is *Columnea banksii* which has pretty naturally trailing evergreen leaves and the added bonus of highly coloured orange flowers during March and April.

An indoor greenhouse creates a warm, moist micro-climate allowing delicate plants to be grown with much more reliable results

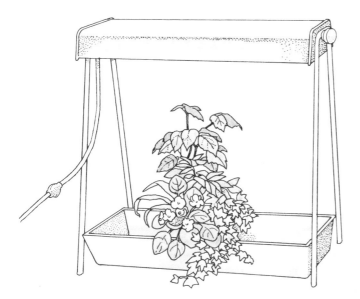

A tabletop lampstand provides light-loving plants such as African violets with the extra boost they need, particularly in wintertime

Artificial lighting

When arranging groups of plants or individual plants indoors, particular care must be taken that the lighting is adequate. A plant stood in a dark corner contributes little to the appearance of the room, yet the same plant artificially lit improves out of all recognition. Use light to enhance the appearance of your plants in the same way as the shopkeeper does to brighten his wares; though with plants, softer lighting is more effective.

Plants at party-time

Here I might well add a further note of warning; at party time plants will be much safer if they are transferred to an upstairs bedroom. Guests who are having just one more drink pressed on them are not above emptying the unwanted alcohol into the convenient receptacle provided by a plant pot! The damage does not become apparent until some time later and the plant's sudden failure usually remains a mystery.

Water-grown plants

The advantage of growing plants by this method, variously referred to as hydroponics or hydroculture amongst other names, is that the amount of water available to the roots of the plant can be fairly accurately controlled. The container in which the plant is growing is provided with a water-level indicator, which makes the task of filling up to the desired level

a reasonably simple operation. With soil-grown plants on the other hand there is always an element of doubt – has the plant had too much, or has it had too little?

There are numerous adaptations of the principle but the majority of plants that are growing in water started their life as conventional soil-grown subjects which, once they were well established, had all the soil washed from around their roots and anchored in the water with special clay pebbles. Those made from London blue clay and known as hydroleca are probably the best type available.

The advantages of these clay pebbles are that they are lightweight, attractive in colour and can absorb about one-third of their own weight of water. When plants are converted from soil-growing to water-growing they are placed in containers that have additional drainage holes in the base to allow maximum movement of water around the roots. When the water level of the container is correctly charged it does not mean that the base of the plant is totally immersed in water, only that the lower three or four inches of the pot, in fact, contain water.

Watering and feeding

When the indicator drops to the minimum mark there is virtually no water around the roots of the plant, but this condition is beneficial rather than harmful, so it is advisable to allow the indicator to remain on the minimum indication for at least three or four days before the reservoir is re-charged. When topping up, ordinary tap water must be used so that the very special fertiliser in the pot can be activated by the chemicals in the water and thus do its work effectively. Known as the ion-exchange fertiliser it is bonded on to polystyrene granules, and as the acidity of the water changes so the fertiliser becomes available to the plant in exactly the right amount. When plants are purchased they will have directions accompanying them which will indicate the frequency with which the fertiliser should be replenished and the amount that is required for the particular container. Because of the chemical interaction between water and fertiliser it is not possible to overfeed plants, but they can be starved of nourishment if one neglects to re-charge with fertiliser at the appropriate time.

All sorts of plants can be grown by means of the hydroponic system, some doing better than others, with flowering plants being the most difficult to manage. Almost all foliage houseplants will succeed, with the aroids, monsteras, philodendrons and similar plants growing at an infinitely quicker pace than the same plants growing more conventionally in soil.

Grouped plants
Besides individual plants in single containers, groups of plants in large troughs (frequently seen in office interiors) will also do splendidly. The important requirement here is that all the individual pots planted in the large container, regardless of the size of the plants, should be placed at the same depth. One can then set the system up with a single water level indicator that will work perfectly as all the pots are sitting in the same level of water.

In winter, for all types of containers the water should be maintained at a slightly lower level than during the summer growing months. Also, in winter it is advisable to use water that is tepid rather than cold, and the growing temperature for the plants should be maintained at a slightly higher average – somewhere in the region of 18°C (65°F).

Changing containers
Transferring plants to larger containers is only necessary if the existing one is very much out of proportion to the size of the plant. The transfer is simply done by lifting the plant out of its existing container and placing it in the larger one, adding sufficient pebbles to ensure that all gaps between the plant roots and the new container are filled in. Be certain that the water indicator is properly located, which means having it at the same depth as it was in the original container.

Converting from soil to water
Besides buying plants that are properly set up for immediate growing there are many kits on the market that will allow you to convert your own plants from soil to water growing. Directions are provided with all of these and some are much more satisfactory than others. However, it is important to ensure that the plants selected for conversion are healthy and well-rooted in the soil, they will then settle to the new growing method much more readily. The other important rule is to ensure that all the soil from around the roots of the plant is removed. This will entail holding the root ball of the plant under running water so that all the roots are exposed and clean. Advice among different kit manufacturers will vary, but the above is important, as is the need for keeping plants warm and shaded while the conversion is taking place.

Having set everything up and got the plants under way it will be found that water-grown plants are very much easier to grow than soil-grown plants.

A cross section of a plant grown on the hydroponic system

CHAPTER 2
Routine culture

Feeding

Beginners with houseplants often launch out with the best intentions, purchasing the best plants, suitable containers, and so on, yet, after a month or two, the plants have much smaller new leaves than they should have, lose their lower ones, and take on a generally hard appearance. Why? In the majority of cases, it is because feeding is being neglected.

The efficient nurseryman sends out established plants, be they in the smallest 'tots' or the larger 10-in size pot. From the time they have become established in their pots, large or small, the plants will have received regular feeding with a balanced fertiliser. Should this supply of nutrient suddenly stop when the plant leaves the nursery, a gradual process of deterioration will take place; hence the smaller and harder leaves.

For the sake of convenience most nurserymen use easily applied liquid fertilisers, though the wise ones occasionally ring the changes and give applications of powdered fertiliser during the growing season.

Simple rules

There are a few simple rules to follow when feeding houseplants. One should ensure that the compost in the pot is moist before applying fertilisers as dry roots are very easily damaged, particularly so if one is misguided enough to use plant food in excess of recommended requirements. Always follow the manufacturers' directions for they have experimented carefully in order to arrive at the correct strength and rate of use for their products. Some plants do not benefit from additional feeding, and advice on this matter is given under the descriptions of individual plants.

Roots are a very important part of almost every plant and any damage caused to the roots will inevitably be reflected sooner or later in the foliage. Damage can frequently be traced to the fact that the soil in the pot has lain wet and sodden for much too long, excluding essential oxygen and causing the roots to rot and die.

By the same token, plants that are fed to excess will also suffer root damage and the inevitable deterioration of the foliage. When a plant is being fed, unless it is very clearly a vigorous subject, the fertiliser manufacturer's feeding directions should be followed. Growth in winter is usually very much slower than in spring and summer, if there is any at all, so caution should be exercised when feeding. Some plants do not require any feeding at this time of year.

On the whole, winter feeding is an unnecessary extravagance, but if a plant produces new leaves in winter it will need a fertiliser that has a low nitrogen content to encourage the production of firm rather than soft leaves. Your sundriesman or florist will be able to advise you on the most suitable one to use.

It is worth experimenting with various fertilisers to see which ones the plants like best. In experimenting you will find out that there is tremendous variety in cost as well as performance.

Foliar feeding
Plants with very vulnerable root systems, the more delicate ferns for example, will respond better to a foliar feed. This is sprayed on to the foliage and assimilated by the plant through the leaves.

When to change the diet
Besides changing the method of feeding in this way, there may also be a need for altering the fertiliser given to the plant at a certain time. For example, many of the flowering pot plants, such as gloxinias, will perform very much better if they have a change of diet as they are about to come into flower. While

leaves are being produced it is necessary to feed established plants with a fertiliser containing a high proportion of nitrogen which will encourage leaf development, and to change to a fertiliser containing a higher proportion of potash at the first sign of flower buds. Therefore a collection containing a mixture of flowering and foliage plants should be fed with fertilisers of differing composition. It all sounds terribly complicated but, in fact, it is a simple matter to purchase what is wanted as all the fertiliser manufacturers clearly list the composition of the feed on the containers.

Tablet fertilisers

Fertilisers in tablet form are also excellent for potted plants and have the advantage of being easy and clean to use. Here again, one should resist the temptation of overdoing it – it is so easy to push into the pot more tablets than recommended by the manufacturer.

Watering

The failure of nearly all the plants that eventually find their way to the dustbin can be traced to the over-indulgent plant enthusiast who is ever ready with the watering can. Strangely enough, it is misguided kindness on the part of the plant owner to feel that the plant needs a little something almost every time he or she has a cup of coffee. Much of the damage can also be attributed to the oft-repeated advice, 'Drop it in a bucket of water, wait until all the bubbles stop coming up and your plant will be sufficiently moist'. To my mind, 'completely waterlogged' would be a better interpretation of the plant's condition.

This treatment may be all very well for the dry azalea, hydrangea, or even the houseplant of the aphelandra type which has been allowed to become very dry, but for the majority of plants it is not advisable. In the greenhouse, however, where moisture in any shape or form is a blessing on a hot day, plunging pots in a bucket of water can have its advantages.

As I travel around the various horticultural shows meeting the gardening or houseplant-growing-public, I am increasingly aware of the need for some sound advice on the subject of watering. Inquirers often say they have purchased a particular plant and would appreciate being told exactly how often it will require watering. I get the impression that an exact answer such as 10.15 a.m. on Tuesday and 3 p.m. on Friday would be quite acceptable. But such a reply would, of course, be ludicrous. Plants are very much like human beings, and no two identical plants reared in similar conditions would require exactly the same treatment in respect of food and liquid nourishment.

So what is the answer? First, there is little doubt that it is best to err on the side of dry conditions rather than wet, and, with the average houseplant, to allow the compost to dry out a little between waterings. Bear in mind that roots in a permanently wet compost become lazy and inactive, there being no need for them to forage in search of moisture. An active root system is the perfect anchor for a well-furnished plant, healthy roots are much more capable of withstanding the indifferent treatment that many indoor plants are often subjected to.

How to tell when plants need water

Often, one is advised to tap the pots with a tool made by fixing a cotton reel on the end of 2-ft cane to test the plants' water requirements. A dry pot will give a resonant ring and a wet pod a dull thud. This piece of advice, handed down through gardening books, may apply where the experienced gardener is concerned, but the mind boggles at the thought of the average owner of a few indoor plants performing this percussion exercise, and trying to decide whether it should be one or two egg-cupfuls of water.

Better by far to give plants a good watering by filling the space between the rim of the pot and the compost each time the soil takes on a dry, grey-brown appearance. If the soil is very dry do this twice, allowing the first lot to soak in before giving the second watering. Err on the side of dryness by all means, but guard against excessively dry soil; the mixture must never be so dry that the compost is coming away from the side of the pot. Should this happen, subsequent watering will result in water finding its way between soil and pot too rapidly, thereby preventing the root ball from becoming moistened which is, after all, the prime object of watering.

A sluggish soil that drains slowly, or not at all, quickly becomes sour. Remedy this by removing the root ball from the pot in order to unblock the drainage holes; it may be necessary to place a few pieces of broken flower pot (crocks) over the drainage holes of clay pots. Plastic pots are amply provided with drainage holes, and only the presence of worms in the soil would cause the drainage holes to become obstructed.

Automatic watering

In recent years the principle of watering plants by means of capillary action has gained many

A capillary watering unit is invaluable to the houseplant-owner at holiday time

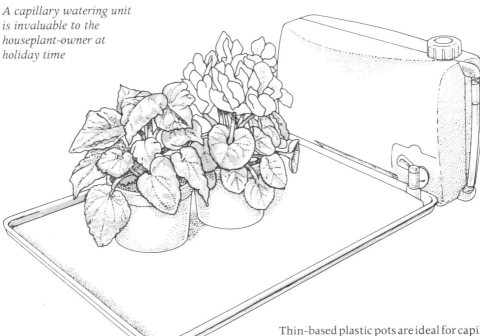

devotees, and much work has been done towards perfecting this method of watering. The plants are stood on a permanently moist base and take up water according to their needs. It is particularly useful if one leads a busy life and cannot attend to the water requirements of plants as often as one should. Equally, it is a boon in the conservatory or greenhouse that is left unattended for most of the day while one is out at work. Capillary watering also presents a method of ensuring that plants have ample moisture at their roots while owners are on holiday. This is particularly useful as houseplants always present a problem at holiday time.

Many plastics' manufacturers have developed trays that need little more than a supply of water from a 'header' tank or bottle, and a 2-in layer of sharp sand or special fibre matting in the tray to become almost foolproof capillary units. The water level in the reservoir tank should be topped up periodically; after initial experiments it becomes a simple matter to adjust the apparatus to ensure that the sand or matting is maintained at the ideal degree of moistness for the plants' needs.

A makeshift capillary unit can be made simply by filling a shallow baking tin with sand and keeping it moist by means of a watering-can. The sand, for best results, should be kept quite wet, but avoid getting the sand into a puddled condition as the plants would suffer from waterlogging and would quickly deteriorate.

Thin-based plastic pots are ideal for capillary watering, as the compost in the pot and the wet sand come into direct contact, thus ensuring that water is drawn up from the sand immediately. Holes in the bottom of clay pots should be plugged with a piece of fibre-glass padding which will act as a wick, so bridging the gap between compost and sand. The plant pots must be gently pushed into the sand when placing them in position. It is important that the soil in the pot should be watered before placing it on the sand to encourage the capillary action. Further watering of the soil should not be necessary.

Lighting

Although some plants will tolerate lower light levels it is generally considered that a minimum of 800 lumens is necessary if plants are to do reasonably well. Better results are possible if a slightly higher level of light can be maintained. The difficulty however is in converting lumens into everyday terms – for example, how many 60 watt light bulbs does one require in order to produce the required light level? Although I have never had a satisfactory answer, it is generally considered that a level of light sufficient to work by is about right for plants. Many plants, African violets (saintpaulias) in particular, will grow perfectly well without any form of daylight if there is adequate artificial lighting for their needs, but it is essential that the lights be left on for at least twelve hours in each twenty-four.

There are specialised light fittings purporting to simulate normal sunshine that one can purchase for placing above plants so that they not only look better, but also grow better. However, for everyday needs the majority of plants will do well in rooms that are bright during the day and augmented by normal room lighting in the evening.

If you are lighting your plants take care not to scorch the leaves. Lights should not be placed too close to plants, particularly spot-lights which generate a considerable amount of heat.

Potting on

One other aspect of houseplant culture that may be taken as routine is the need to transfer plants to larger containers when the soil becomes exhausted. The appearance of a few wispy roots through the bottom of the pot does not necessarily indicate that the plant is in need of fresh soil. The actual root ball must be inspected by removing the plant from its pot, and if the roots are well matted you may then consider that potting on is necessary. An emphatic plea – plants should not be knocked out of their pots any more than is absolutely necessary. A friend describes it as resembling a surgical operation from which the plant requires time to recover.

The potting on operation is best performed in March or April when the roots are starting into active growth and will quickly get on the move into the new compost.

Pot sizes
Pots are available in many sizes, but in the business of growing plants commercially the larger sizes are generally 5-, 7- and 10-inch; thereafter plants go into a tub of one kind or another.

The potting sequence is geared to the sizes of pot that are generally available: you transfer a plant from a 5-in pot to a 7-in pot and when it has outgrown the 7-in pot you simply put it into a 10-in container. Once established in pots of this size, the majority of indoor plants will be happy for many years if regular feeding is not neglected.

Potting composts
The potting mixture itself is not so critical as we are sometimes led to believe. Experience has shown that almost all houseplants prefer a light, open soil of a spongy texture. To arrive at this, without suggesting ingredients that are often difficult to acquire, use a mix consisting of two-thirds John Innes No. 2 potting compost (or No. 3 for larger pots) and one-third clean peat. Naturally enough, some plants will

need a different mixture; these will be dealt with in the notes on individual plants.

With the increase in popularity of indoor plants there has been an inevitable increase in the supply and range of ancillary items that are available to improve the performance or

A simple method of potting on: use the existing pot as a mould to make a hole in the new soil exactly the right size for the rootball of the plant

appearance of the plant. One pleasing result of this activity is that there is now a much wider range of potting mediums from which to choose – soil for acid- and lime-loving plants, soil for cacti and soilless composts.

Soilless composts

The last mentioned are composed almost entirely of peat with added nutrients. Much experimentation has gone on in perfecting these soilless mixes, and they are excellent for a wide range of indoor plants, provided one ensures that the feeding of the plant is never neglected. It is also important that these composts are never allowed to dry out excessively as they are difficult to re-wet satisfactorily. Perhaps I am a little old fashioned, but I am still a little hesitant when it comes to using soilless mixes for larger plants that are to stay in the same pot for a long time. I feel that such plants require a percentage of loam in the potting mixture, but for smaller plants the soilless mixes offer quite considerable advantages.

A technique for beginners

For the experienced gardener potting is a simple enough task, but the beginner may well approach it with some misgiving. The novice might benefit by adopting the following method; instead of potting the actual plant, take a pot of the same size as that in which your plant is growing and use if to form a mould in the slightly larger container. It is then a simple task to remove the plant from its pot and drop it into the perfectly shaped hole, having first removed the empty pot.

Potting on larger plants

Most growers of indoor plants will happily tackle the task of potting on small plants into larger pots but tend to be less adventurous when it comes to moving large plants on into more roomy containers. Yet the principles involved are very much the same – the new pot should be only a little larger than the one the plant is growing in, and both the plant and new compost should be moist. Spring is the best time to tackle the job. However, the actual time of year is not critical if the growing conditions are favourable.

Potting of larger plants can be undertaken in exactly the same way as that described for smaller plants – you simply make a mould in the new compost with the pot that the plant is growing in, and then place the root ball of the plant in the perfectly shaped hole. However it is of the utmost importance to ensure that the soil is well firmed around the root ball before giving a thorough watering.

Cleaning the leaves

Many indoor plant growers have a fetish for cleaning the leaves of their charges when, more often than not, the plant would be much happier if it were left alone. Wiping the leaves of plants with a soft, damp cloth is quite adequate most of the time; care must be taken not to handle tender new leaves. There are all sorts of concoctions on the market for imparting a gloss to the leaves of indoor plants, but all of them must be used sparingly and with a degree of discrimination. You must never use leaf cleaning sprays or liquids when temperatures are low, or if plants are likely to be exposed to direct sunlight immediately afterwards. When making use of any leaf cleaner for the first time it is advisable to test it on one hidden leaf first in case it damages the leaves in any way.

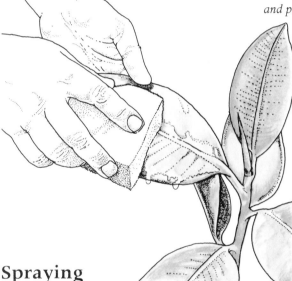

Large-leaved plants need an occasional wash with clear water to remove dust and particles of grime

Spraying

Many indoor plants, particularly those that prefer high humidity such as ferns, will relish an occasional fine spray of water on their leaves. Besides offering beneficial humidity, the presence of moisture will deter red spider mite which thrives in hot, dry conditions. When spraying plants with water, and especially when treating with an insecticide, particular care must be taken to ensure that the undersides of leaves are thoroughly wetted.

A further word of warning, particularly important where aerosol sprays are much in use, is that one should at no time expose plants to housefly sprays, furniture polish aerosols, or hair lacquer sprays. In fact, indoor plants must at all times be protected from all forms of spray other than those that are specifically intended for use on plants.

CHAPTER 3
Types of container

The makers of fancy pots, troughs and such like have not been slow in keeping abreast of the general increase of interest in houseplants in recent years. A wide range of designs and materials are available for this purpose.

When selecting containers the appearance is, of course, important, but it is also essential to ensure that they are of adequate size and that they are watertight. To obviate the possibility of water seepage damaging furniture, one should take the precaution of placing a cork mat under the container until it is obvious that dampness is not likely to be a problem.

Wooden containers

In spite of all the new materials, plant troughs and boxes made from good quality timber still hold their own and blend perfectly with almost any kind of foliage. Such boxes can be made watertight by inserting a metal liner, or, more cheaply and simply, by using drawing pins to tack a double thickness of polythene to the inside of the box. When using any form of wood preservative for treating boxes prior to planting, care must be taken to ensure that the material is not harmful to plant life.

In most cases it will be advisable to fit legs to the container or to place it on a table where plants may benefit from the maximum light available, only larger plants should actually be placed on the floor. The fitting of castors enables one to move plant boxes back into the warmth of the room in the evening where the plants will be much more comfortable than they would be if left in the cooler window position.

Dish-type containers

I find that dish-type containers of fairly generous proportions (deep enough to accommodate a 5-in pot) are excellent for temporary plant arrangements. The owner of a dozen or so plants will derive much pleasure from displaying them in a group as a change from lining the windowsill or decorating the wall. If the container is first filled with peat, newspaper, or sphagnum moss, which is kept moist, this will ensure that plants remain firmly in position when inserted. One precaution is necessary: do not allow the plants to be too congested. There must be sufficient space between each for them to be individually appreciated. Displays of this kind can be dismantled and rearranged weekly and will permit the use of flowering pot plants when they are in season, thus providing an extra touch of colour.

Plant troughs

The majority of houseplants seem to enjoy the company of each other, and grow better when they are grouped together. However, the large plant that is well-established will happily endure solitude in its individual corner.

Plants grouped together in a plant trough, provide a pleasing focal point in the room, besides affording the plants more agreeable conditions in which to grow. Where possible, plants ought to stand on, or be plunged in, a moisture-retaining material of some kind. Sphagnum moss, moist peat, or even wet newspaper can be used for this purpose. So that watering needs can be attended to, care must be taken to ensure that the pots are plunged only to their rims and no further. Moist pebbles, or one of the light-weight aggregates such as Lytag, provide an ideal base for standing pots on. Though pebbles must be kept wet to give a moist atmosphere around plants, it will be detrimental if the plant pot is actually allowed to stand in water.

Other suggestions

Try exploring local junk and antique shops for suitable containers such as pretty china washing bowls. It is also possible to obtain antique or reproduction versions of the Victorian jardinière which consists of an elegant pedestal topped with a matching bowl.

Copper soup tureens and old brass coal scuttles, if they can be acquired, are also excellent for setting off groups of indoor plants.

Self-watering pots

Houseplant owners who are obliged to leave their plants unattended for any length of time may well gain from purchasing one of the variety of self-watering pots and troughs that are on the market. Not all of these give the desired results, but the majority, having overcome their teething troubles, are now thoroughly reliable. With these devices,

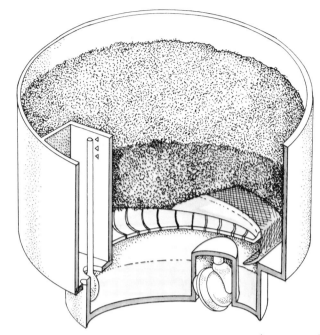

An automatic watering pot. Being clean and easy to move about, these are ideal for office arrangements

Junk shops and markets will prove to be fertile hunting grounds for unusual plant containers

watering is simplified to the point where one merely tops up the water supply at intervals to a clearly marked level. Such containers are also ideal for the plant grower who is at a loss to know what to do with indoor plants when going on holiday. Recently, I heard about a rubber plant that grew in a self-watering pot from a height of 2 ft to 9 ft in the space of three years. This remarkable rate of growth was, it seems, achieved with the minimum amount of attention.

Spiral planters look attractive from any angle but watering must be done carefully

Tall containers

Strawberry pots, made of clay with carefully placed holes in their sides for plants, can be especially attractive when planted up with a collection of different ivies with something more colourful such as a geranium planted in the top of the pot.

Tower pots are similar, but slightly more elaborate; these are plastic cylinders with bays for plants in their sides that can be stacked one top of the other. The cylinder is filled with compost, and as this is being done plants are introduced through the gaps in the side of the container. In limited space this is an excellent way of growing all sorts of indoor plants to make the most of their varied colours and habits. Tower pots are also suitable for growing strawberries in a limited space such as a patio or balcony.

Wall brackets

One sometimes sees photographs of interiors in magazines in which exotic houseplants are displayed to perfection. On seeing the latter, the reader may be tempted to set forth and purchase an exotically-coloured codiaeum (croton) for placing in a wall bracket where it will blend perfectly with the general decor. The hot, dry atmosphere that plants will have to contend with when pinned to the wall will, in most instances, result in quite rapid deterioration.

If neglected for only a short time the leaves of the wall plant will quickly take on a dry, toasted appearance. When positioning wall brackets it is particularly important to ensure that they are not directly over room heaters; the hot dry air from these would lessen the plant's chance of survival. Tiny pots dry out very rapidly, so ensure that you buy brackets which will accommodate a pot of at least $3\frac{1}{2}$-in diameter so that the plants in them can be thoroughly watered.

Wall brackets, in my opinion, are not suitable for the majority of houseplants, except for the real toughies, such as ivies, tradescantias, *Philodendron scandens* and *Rhoicissus rhomboidea*. Less hardy plants should be placed where their needs can be more readily administered to, and, unless of trailing habit, the majority of smaller plants are really seen to best effect when one looks down on them.

Wall brackets are decoratively pleasing but only reasonably hardy plants should be used in them

1. *Sit the hanging basket in the top of a large pot to make watering easier*
2. *Line the basket with sphagnum moss and fill the bottom with compost*
3. *Carefully place some of the plants through the sides of the basket and firm their roots into the compost*
4. *Fill the remainder of the basket with compost*
5. *Position the final plants in the top of the basket remembering to allow room for them to grow and develop naturally*
6. *A hanging basket planted-up with colourful summer-flowering plants will provide a long-lasting source of pleasure for a patio or conservatory*

Hanging baskets

Many of the easier houseplants will benefit from a short 'holiday' in the garden during the summer months. In this connection the hanging basket is ideal in that it can be planted and put in position outside in the garden or on the balcony and can be quickly moved to a sheltered spot should the weather become inclement.

Planting up a hanging basket
The basket you choose should have a reasonably close mesh and not be rusted or damaged. Fresh, moist sphagnum moss should be used to line it. Place the basket in a large empty pot for support and then tease out the moss to make an even lining without gaps. Fill the basket with the chosen compost (preferably peat-based) and firm it into position as you go along. If desired, small trailing plants, such as ivy, tradescantia and lobelia, can be planted through the sides of the basket so that a fuller effect is achieved when the planting is complete. When the basket is filled with firmly compressed compost the principal plants can then be introduced. This is simply done by making large enough holes in the compost to receive the root ball of each plant in turn. One should avoid the temptation to plant too thickly, as plants in baskets that are kept moist and fed regularly will usually make rapid progress.

If the basket is intended for the conservatory, patio, or the greenhouse there is a very wide range of plants to choose from: lobelia that will trail down, petunias in an incredible range of colour, geraniums both upright and trailing, ivies and fuchsias. Although they may be included with other plants I find that fuchsias are much more satisfactory when individual varieties, such as *Fuchsia* Cascade or *F.* Marinka (both natural trailing types), are the only plants in the basket. For indoor use, however, one should confine the choice of plants to those that are known to do well in the home – fuchsias for example would be of no value as there is not sufficient light indoors for these plants to retain their flowers.

Although one must agree that the conventional moss-lined basket is probably best, excellent results can be had by lining the basket with black polythene prior to filling with compost and planting. Some form of drainage is essential, so use a skewer to perforate the polythene after planting. Where drips may be a problem there are baskets available with built-in trays.

CHAPTER 4
Easily grown houseplants

Over the years the majority of the plants referred to in this chapter have proved successful in all manner of conditions, and almost all are available from a general nurseryman. Purchase of some will, however, necessitate a special order to your supplier, and the possibility of having to wait until a batch of plants becomes available.

Growing conditions and cultural directions for plants in this group can be generalised; where special treatment is required this is stated in my notes on individual plants. On the whole, a light position and a temperature in the region of 16°C (60°F) is advised. Information on general care (watering, feeding and such like) will be found in the chapter on Routine culture.

To make reference easy, the plants in this section have been grouped together in their families. There is also a comprehensive index at the back of the book.

Araceae

Aroid family
Plants belonging to the family *Araceae* are frequently referred to as aroids, and they are to be found almost everywhere in the world in one form or another. The arum lily is one of the best known members of this botanical grouping.

If houseplant growers were to be deprived of any particular family of plants, for some reason or other, one feels that the aroids would be their greatest loss. From this single family we get easy plants, difficult ones, flowering plants, and many of the bolder ones so much relied upon for display and general decoration. Almost all of the pot-grown members prefer a temperature in excess of 16°C (60°F) and the atmosphere is rarely too humid for them. Yet

one recalls the disastrous cold winter of 1962–63 when many plants were obliged to suffer lower temperatures than were previously thought possible. Although many succumbed, a surprising number pulled through. We learned that when low temperatures were unavoidable the plants tolerated the conditions much more satisfactorily when the soil in the pot was kept almost bone dry. One batch of *Philodendron bipinnatifidum* that we were growing, when treated in this way, survived temperatures that were, on many nights, down to 1°C (34°F).

Monstera deliciosa borsigiana
Swiss cheese plant
Really mature plants of monstera would in some cases be large enough to fill a small living room, leaving very little space for inhabitants or furniture. Do not be alarmed, when confined to smaller pots indoors, the leaves remain a manageable size.

Often I am asked what one should do with the freely produced aerial roots of this plant. The answer is to tie them in loosely with string and wind them around on top of the soil in the pot. Make a hole in the compost with a pencil and direct the tip of the root into it; this will keep the young roots under control.

One must be patient in order to appreciate the reason for the name *deliciosa*, as there is nothing about the plant itself to suggest the reason for it. Mature plants of monstera will in time produce exquisite, creamy-white inflorescences (flowerheads). These are very short lived and eventually develop into fruits of the most unappetising appearance. To sample the fruit at its best one must be patient and leave it on the plant until the outer protective covering begins to disintegrate. Even then it is possible to eat only a little of the fruit at a time, with its elusive pineapple-banana flavour; in Australia it is called the

continued on page 44

The
Living Room

The living room probably offers more scope for growing
houseplants than any other room in the house as it is likely
to be both light and warm. Plants on a windowsill look fine
during the day but on winter's evenings bring them into
the room rather than leave them trapped in the cold air
between window and curtain. A fireplace arrangement
makes a good feature for a living room **(below)** as long as
draughts can be excluded. Blinds rather than curtains
make a room beautifully light **(right)** so that a wide range of
plants can be grown.

fruit salad plant. I find that it is best to stand the fruit in a jug and to eat a little with a spoon each day as the outer green covering goes through the natural process of peeling itself away from the pulp-like fruit underneath. Do not let the appearance of the edible part put you off – your courage will be well rewarded.

Monstera leaves can be cleaned in the same way as those of other glossy-leaved plants, though great care must be taken not to handle young leaves, which are very easily damaged.

Philodendron bipinnatifidum

This plant is best suited to the more spacious room where its large leaves will have an opportunity to extend to their full spread. Though sometimes offered for sale, smaller plants are not very satisfactory, as the leaves do not show their true character until the plants are growing freely in pots of at least 7-in in diameter.

Surprisingly enough, I once saw this plant being used as a hanging basket subject in one of the reception areas of a continental airport. It is comparatively easy to grow so maintenance was little bother, and the plant effectively relieved the emptiness of the high ceiling.

There are several similar philodendrons with leaves radiating from a central crown on petioles 2 ft or more in length. These will develop aerial roots in time and, as an alternative to tying them together on top of the pot, the roots can be directed into a container of water and allowed to take in moisture from this source. It is also a good way of interesting young children in plants for they will be intrigued to see the root action. When a plant is treated in this way it will be found that the compost in the pot requires comparatively little water.

Philodendron Burgundy and P. hastatum

These two plants are both typical of the aroid family in their cultural needs. Both benefit if their supporting stakes are clad with a 1- or 2-in layer of fresh sphagnum moss. If the moss is kept moist, the freely produced aerial roots will quickly find their way into it, and the plant will grow much better as a result. Keeping mossed stakes moist indoors does, however, present a problem. This may be overcome by standing the plant in the bath, or outdoors (on a fine day), and thoroughly soaking the moss with a hand spray. Many of the other aroids will also benefit from the use of similar mossed stakes. These stakes are easily prepared by binding the moss to the stake with plastic-covered wire of neutral colour; plastic wire is preferable to metal wire as it is non-corrosive.

Philodendron scandens, the popular sweetheart plant

Damp sphagnum moss bound firmly to a stake with rust-proof wire is the best form of support for moisture-loving plants

Philodendron scandens
Sweetheart plant

By far the best known of the philodendrons is *P. scandens*, or the sweetheart plant; this is mainly because of its ability to withstand ill-treatment. It would be nice to say it remains unscathed, but low temperatures and mishandling soon give the leaves a dry, paper-like appearance instead of their natural glossy green. The American common name, bathroom plant, gives a clue to the conditions it likes – a hot and steamy atmosphere. Bathrooms with a minimum temperature of 16°C (60°F) are ideal; it would be unwise to subject *P. scandens* to the temperature fluctuations of the average bathroom which is often very cold for most of the day. Fluctuating temperatures are more damaging to plants than those that are constant, even though slightly below the recommended level.

Araliaceae

Aralia family

Plants belonging to the *Araliaceae*, the aralia family, are native to both tropical and temperate parts of the world and include many with ornamental foliage and attractive habit.

Fatsia japonica and Fatshedera lizei variegata

When considering this family we are immediately faced with a plant that masquerades under two names – *Fatsia japonica* and *Aralia sieboldii*. Like the ivies, which also belong to this family, the aralias are dual-purpose plants in that they may be planted out in a sheltered spot in the garden when they have outgrown their allotted space indoors or as an alternative to throwing them in the dustbin. The green form of *Fatsia japonica* is an 'easy doer' that will, with proper attention, make a substantial plant, though this will take some time in room conditions.

In common with almost all variegated plants, *F. japonica variegata* is a slightly more difficult plant that is inclined to have brown leaf edges if neglected. Larger plants of this variety will remain more compact and attractive if they are potted into standard John Innes No. 3 potting compost.

Before discussing the ivies, I must mention a man-made plant, fatshedera, which gets its name from its two parents, fatsia and hedera. Having enlarged ivy-shaped leaves on the upright stem, the fatshedera is an excellent choice for the back row of a group of plants. *Fatshedera lizei variegata*, the variegated variety, is a more colourful plant, but inclined

continued on page 48

Overleaf A varied collection of easily grown houseplants
1   *Sansevieria trifasciata laurentii*
2   *Chlorophytum comosum*
3   *Rhoicissus rhomboidea*
4   Two varieties of peperomia
5   *Billbergia windii*
6   *Philodendron scandens* and *Pilea* Moon Valley
7   *Maranta leuconeura erythrophylla*

Fatshedera lizei

to have brown leaf edges if the compost is kept permanently wet.

For those with an experimental turn of mind it is interesting to try grafting one of the more decorative small-leaved hederas onto the top of a fatshedera, thus giving a fascinating plant that will never fail to interest visitors. To perform the grafting operation it is necessary to have a reasonably healthy fatshedera plant about 3 to 4 ft in height, which should have its growing tip removed. The stem should be attached to a cane to keep it erect. With a sharp knife cut down twice into the stem just above the leaf joint for about 1 in. Prepare four wedge-shaped ivy tip cuttings from firm pieces, and insert these into the cross-shaped cut made in the top of the fatshedera. Tie them very firmly in position with raffia or adhesive tape, place a polythene bag over them and tie the bag in position. The bag will prevent the cuttings drying out and will consequently help them to bond much more readily. When the cuttings begin to grow the bag must be removed and when the ivy pieces have developed several new leaves the tips should be pinched out to encourage a bushy appearance.

1. *The growing tip of the plant is removed and a cross cut made into the stem*
2. *The ivy tip cuttings are placed in the cross cut*
3. *The cuttings are bound tightly into place with raffia and the whole graft is covered with a polythene bag*

4. *The resulting plant when ivy growth has matured and the leaves of the original fatshedera plant have been stripped off*

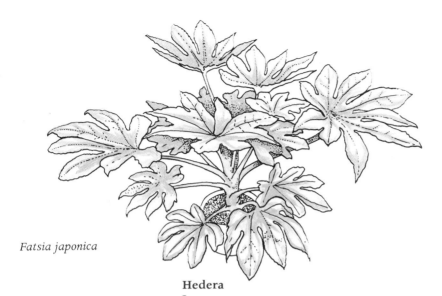

Fatsia japonica

Hedera
Ivy

In spite of flowering plants, exotic foliaged ones and new introductions, the hederas, or ivies, still retain their popularity, and can well form an interesting specialised collection of plants. In fact, a collection of ivies would give a pleasing display all the year around. There are about 25 different kinds to choose from, though only about 15 are readily available.

We hear many opinions to the contrary, but it has been my experience that all the ivies offered for sale as houseplants also make excellent garden plants. Success in establishing them out of doors depends to some extent on the planting time. Give the soil time to warm up, then, about the middle of May, plant them out. On walls, in the rock garden, or dotted around in the shrub border they will be a continual source of pleasure. By far the most spectacular is *Hedera canariensis* and, when planted against a sheltered wall, there can be few climbing plants that give a better year-round display. Some I planted a few years ago were reluctant to produce anything more than the odd bit of straggling growth until two substantial York paving stones were placed on the soil immediately in front of them. The cool, moist root run under the stones seemed to be exactly what the doctor ordered. Grown in this way there should never be any shortage of cream and green material for flower arrangements.

Even when the last spark of life appears to have deserted your ivy, put it in the garden instead of the bin – the results, nine times out of ten, will surprise you.

But the subject is indoor plants, to which I return. Of the larger-leaved ivies probably *H. canariensis* and *H. maculata* are the most popular; others, such as the varieties Raven-holst and Gold Leaf, have fallen out of favour. Indoors, ivies all require similar conditions for

success – the most important being a light, airy room and a modest temperature in the region of 13°C (55°F). Hot and dry conditions encourage red spider mite; the browning of leaf edges is by way of being their trade mark.

Almost all growers of houseplants list a good selection of hederas, so there would not seem to be any need for repeating them all here. However, some of my particular favourites are worthy of special mention.

Hedera helix Adam has grey-green variegation and tiny leaves which are perfectly shaped and compactly arranged on the stem to the point where they overlap on particularly good specimens. Because of the tightly matted leaves, care must be taken not to get the centre of the plant too wet, or wet at all for that matter. It will also pay to periodically check over the plants and remove any dead leaves that would be liable to rot if left in the centre. The compact leaves and distinct variegation make this variety a great favourite with florists as the final touch to brides' bouquets.

Stocks of the variety Little Diamond vary considerably in quality, so care must be taken when making one's selection to ensure that the individual leaves are, as the name suggests, diamond shaped. Good stock should also have naturally twisting stems, and such plants are particularly suitable for grafting on top of fatshedera, as previously described.

I am including the variety Glacier not so much for its attractiveness as for its lasting qualities. For inclusion in an arrangement of plants, to trail over the edge of the container and break its line, Glacier is ideal. It is also particularly suitable for use as a trailing plant in window-boxes out of doors and does not seem to mind harsh weather.

The small-leaved ivies almost all branch freely when the growing tips have been removed; this should be done occasionally to keep the plants compact and tidy. One of the exceptions is Jubilee (commonly named Golden Heart on account of its gold-centred leaves with a green perimeter), and for this reason it is not often grown commercially. In full sun in the rock garden, however, it can be relied upon to give a good year-round display, for although there is a tendency to wander, growth is easily snipped back and kept under control.

The easily grown *H. canariensis* is quite the best of those with bolder leaves. One of its drawbacks is its unwillingness to branch when the growing tip is removed. Instead it continues to grow from the leaf bud immediately below the position where the tip was taken out. So, in order to keep the plant within bounds, the growth should be wound back and forth

continued on page 52

Despite their exotic appearance most bromeliads are not difficult to care for. Often the colourful bract will last for many months so, although they are by no means cheap, they are good value for money
Left The stunning bract of *Guzmania lindenii*
Above right *Neoregelia carolinae tricolor*
Right *Aechmea rhodocyanea*

around itself. When twisting the stems, take the simple precaution of bending them in a gentle arch, for if the growth is bent at too acute an angle the flow of sap is checked and the part beyond the fractured stem invariably dies off.

Bromeliaceae

Bromeliad or pineapple family
Named after the Swedish botanist, Bromel, members of the *Bromeliaceae* or pineapple family, are much neglected. If only on account of their durability, they deserve to be more popular.

It is always a problem to decide whether the bromeliads should be included among the flowering plants or the foliage plants, but as most of them take several years to produce flowers (some as many as fifteen) I feel that they are with us longer as foliage rather than as flowering plants, and have included them here.

Billbergia
Billbergia is surely one of the easiest of all indoor plants to care for, the most popular varieties being *B. nutans* with narrow leaves and *B. windii* that has broader leaves. There

Billbergia nutans

are several others that display very exotic bracts, but all for only a few days duration. All have the typical elongated funnel-shaped bracts of the billbergia from which emerge more bracts of exotic colouring.

Both *B. nutans* and *B. windii* will form solid clumps of rosettes in time, which can be divided at any time to provide new plants. Plant divided pieces into small pots filled with peaty compost and they should produce greenish coloured bracts in a surprisingly short time. Plants with their roots bound in a clump of sphagnum moss and attached to a tree branch in the greenhouse can present a most impressive sight when the pendulous bracts appear. Given reasonable temperature and conditions they are dependable plants.

Cryptanthus
Earth stars
Beginning with the smallest members of the family, there are the cryptanthuses and tillandsias; the latter has an exciting range of bract shapes and flowers, mostly in shades of blue, but these are short-lived. For the bottle garden there can be no better choice than the compact cryptanthuses that can remain undisturbed for long periods without attention. These are grown primarily for their colouring, and, perhaps more particularly, for their fascinating shapes that have earned for them the apt common name of earth stars.

The flowers of the cryptanthuses are, on the whole, insignificant and barely emerge from the tightly overlapping leaves of the plants. In common with other members of the family, offsets will be produced at soil level when flowering has finished. When large enough these offsets can be removed by bending them to one side, and can be planted up individually in small pots filled with a peaty mixture. Rooting will be considerably speeded up if the pots are stood on a bed of peat which has an electric soil-warming cable running through it.

Cryptanthus tricolor, unfortunately rather a costly plant, is of striking appearance, particularly when the cream and green striped leaves take on a reddish tint. Both the colouring and appearance of *C. tricolor* is greatly improved when the plants are grown in a natural way on an old log or piece of bark, instead of in the more conventional pot. These 'mobiles', as they are called, have a certain fascination when suspended in mid-air on a length of clear nylon fishing line. Only close inspection will convince admirers that the 'object' is not floating in space.

Mobiles are easily made by knocking plants from their pots and placing a wad of fresh sphagnum moss around the exposed roots; the

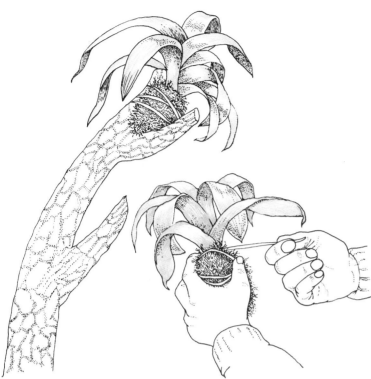

light and dark shades of grey, form an urn-shaped rosette, the centre of which must be kept topped up with water. From the centre of the 'urn' the bold pink bract emerges, and from the bract striking blue flowers eventually appear. The cost of these plants often discourages the would-be purchaser, but it should be borne in mind that they very rarely take less than four years to produce a bract. With the assistance of carefully measured chemicals and gases, plants can be induced to flower in less time; the results, however, rarely match up to the naturally produced product.

Ideally, aechmeas should be purchased when the bract is a little above the water level in the urn. Records show that, when purchased at this stage, it is quite possible for them to remain colourful for up to 12 months. As the bract begins to fade and die, so too, does the rosette from which it came; this is common to all bromeliads. When the main rosette is no longer attractive it should be cut away with a sharp knife, care being taken not to damage the new young shoots that will by then be sprouting from the base of the parent plant.

moss ball is then tied securely to the chosen anchorage. Nails can be driven into the bark or log and used for tying the plants, and these can subsequently be concealed by an additional bit of moss wedged in around them. Needless to say, mobiles are better suited to the greenhouse or conservatory where drips resulting from watering will not be a problem. Water the plants by saturating the moss with a fine syringe when necessary, or by plunging the plant and anchorage in a bucket of tepid water.

Some of the tillandsias will also be perfectly happy if attached to a log in this way, though care must be exercised to ensure that only those with small, compact rosettes are selected.

Epiphytic plants grow well if their roots are wrapped in sphagnum moss and bound to the branch of a tree or piece of bark

Larger Bromeliads

Space permits mention of only a few of the larger bromeliads, *Aechmea rhodocyanea, Guzmania lindenii, Neoregelia carolinae tricolor* and *Vriesea splendens*. All are spectacular plants that should give little difficulty if a minimum temperature of 16°C (60°F) can be maintained.

Aechmea rhodocyanea
Urn plant

Aechmea rhodocyanea is a very fine plant, and one that the uninformed look at with amazement, wondering whether it is real or not. They might well wonder, for a mature plant with a well-developed flowering bract has few competitors in the 'exotic honours' field. Large, strap-like, recurving leaves, banded in

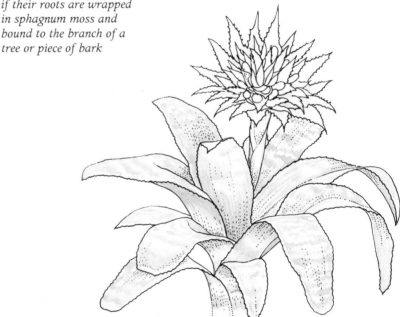

Aechmea rhodocyanea

There is much argument as to whether or not one should remove these shoots and pot them up individually, or leave them to develop still attached to the parent rosette. I can only quote the experience of a keen gardener of my acquaintance, who was in fact the part-time gardener at my local railway station. He left the cluster of five 'pups' on his plant, and two years later he had the most magnificent specimen with four heads at the

continued on page 56

Far right This plant display has been put together to contrast many different leaf shapes and colours. It includes *Begonia rex*, *Maranta leuconeura kerchoveana* (rabbit's tracks), *Philodendron scandens* and heptapleurum
Top right Coleus is easy to propagate and provides a wealth of colourful plants
Bottom right Two plants with interesting leaf markings: *Peperomia magnoliaefolia and Pilea cadierei*

peak of perfection, all in full colour at the same time. What is more, they were still in the same soil. Why did number five fail to develop? There is always a 'why' in gardening!

In the greenhouse, healthy plants will produce side growths that develop quickly and may have bracts in as little as one year, but this is the exception and two years at least must be allowed under normal circumstances.

With all larger bromeliads it is important that the 'urn' be kept topped up with water, preferably clean rain water which should be completely changed periodically to prevent it becoming stagnant.

Guzmania lindenii

Another bromeliad which is spectacular when the head of dark red bracts appears is *Guzmania lindenii*. It needs a warm, but lightly shaded position and, as with other bromeliads, the compost should be only just moist but the vase in the centre must be filled with water.

Other good kinds include the much smaller *G. lingulata minor* with orange-coloured bracts and a new sort, *G.* Orangeade, with orange bracts and pale green leaves.

Neoregelia carolinae tricolor

Neoregelia carolinae tricolor is another spectacular and thoroughly reliable plant which I first saw growing in an airport restaurant where the amount of natural daylight was negligible. In fact, the neoregelia was one of only two survivors from the original planting – in spite of the fact that the 'urn' seemed to provide a convenient receptacle for discarded cigarette ends.

The saw-edged overlapping leaves will brighten any display with their cream and green variegation; strong sunlight will give an overall russet flush to the leaves. Mature plants eventually have bright red centres, and at the same time the rather insignificant flowering bract appears in the middle of the urn, barely emerging from the water that must always be present. A word of caution, as the flowers appear the water in the urn takes on an unpleasant odour and should be changed more frequently than usual. The compost in the pot must be kept moist, but never saturated. Many of the bromeliads will tolerate comparatively dry root conditions provided the water level in the urn is maintained, but the lower leaves of the neoregelia become brown and shrivelled if the soil is excessively dry for any length of time.

Vriesea splendens

The vrieseas include some of the most interesting plants in the family. In particular there are *Vriesea hieroglyphica* and *V. fenestralis*, both of which have astonishingly intricate leaf markings. These I mention only by way of interest, knowing that they are difficult to acquire, and that only the true expert could ever hope to succeed with them indoors.

Vriesea splendens is a plant that is generally available and relatively easy to care for. It should have a light position in the room. An interesting feature of this plant is the way in which the transverse light and dark bands of colour on the leaves gradually blend into a greenish-brown overall colouring as the spear-shaped red bract increases in size.

Compost for bromeliads

Bromeliads, on the whole, have rather poor root systems, so when potting it is important to ensure that a light, open compost is used. One successful mixture consists of the following ingredients: one-third pine needles, one-third oak or birch leafmould, and one-third peat. If all those materials are not at hand, prepare a mixture which conforms to this specification as nearly as possible, bearing in mind the need for an open, spongy compost.

Commelinaceae

Spiderwort family

The *Commelinaceae* or spiderwort family is native to tropical and subtropical regions and includes the tradescantias, which will be familiar to many readers.

Zebrina pendula

Tradescantia Quicksilver

Tradescantia

Wandering Jew

There is always a soft spot for one or other of the tradescantia tribe, first introduced to this country some 300 years ago and still as popular as ever. Most are easy to care for, while others are a wee bit difficult; almost all of them root like the proverbial weed when propagated from cuttings. For the beginner there can be no better choice than tradescantias, and the many varieties available will ensure a pleasing range of colour throughout the year.

In the easier range there are the varieties Silver, Gold, *tricolor, purpurea* and the lovely Quick Silver, which has altogether larger and more colourful leaves. *Zebrina pendula*, formerly named *Tradescantia zebrina*, with silver, green, purple and grey leaves, is another in the easy range. Slightly more difficult are *T. blossfeldiana variegata, T. quadricolor* and the related *Setcreasea purpurea*, the purple heart.

Many are the complaints we hear of tradescantias turning green in colour and losing their bright appearance; much of this is due to inadequate light and too much moisture at the roots. The old adage that tradescantias should be kept dry and starved in order to preserve the variegation has never proved itself in my experience; such treatment results in thin, weedy growth that may be variegated but is certainly never attractive. Stand them in the lightest possible window, feed them regularly and pot them on as required is the best advice for obtaining healthy and variegated plants. Also, when green shoots appear on the plant they should be ruthlessly removed, as these contain much more chlorophyll and so grow more rapidly, leading to a completely green plant in time.

One is often shown a tradescantia with the proud comment that the plant is four, five or even six years old; and, quite honestly, they almost all look as if they are at least that age. To get the best out of these plants, new ones should be started each year in order to provide fresh, vigorous growth. Select the most colourful growths, about 4 in in length, and put five or six around the edge of a 3½-in pot filled with John Innes No. 2 potting compost or a soilless equivalent. Rooting them first in a normal propagating mixture is a complete waste of time. To keep the plants compact, the cuttings should have their growing tips removed almost as soon as they have rooted.

Where space permits, it may be worthwhile preparing a hanging basket of tradescantias. Do this by selecting half-a-dozen potfuls of the most colourful plants and space them out evenly in a basket that has been lined with black polythene and filled with John Innes No. 2 potting compost or a soilless equivalent. It is important that the polythene should have several holes made in it so that excess water can drain away easily. Tie in some of the longer shoots underneath the basket and pinch out the growing tips periodically to improve the shape of the plant; weed out those green shoots as they appear. The *tricolor* and Silver varieties make particularly good subjects for use in baskets.

Setcreasea purpurea
Purple heart

Setcreasea purpurea belongs to the same tribe as the much more common tradescantias, but it is a much more difficult plant to track down when it comes to purchasing as well as being marginally more difficult to care for.

The striped leaves have a base colour of olive green, and are an attractive purple on the undersides; the small white flowers of the plant are insignificant. Useful as a hanging plant, it will quickly develop masses of long, trailing growth in conditions offering reasonable light and warmth. New plants can be raised from cuttings a few inches in length taken at almost any time of the year. Plants should be fed regularly while in active growth, and the soil should never be allowed to become wet and sodden.

Compositae

Daisy family

The *Compositae* or daisy family provides us with many of our most colourful and adaptable garden plants, and the potential of many as pot plants has not been neglected. Both of the plants mentioned here are grown primarily for their foliage, as their flowers are comparatively insignificant.

Gynura sarmentosa

Gynura sarmentosa
Dead nettle

This plant attracts the eye, especially when the sunlight picks out the velvety purple colouring of the topmost leaves. Reasonably easy to grow, *Gynura sarmentosa* may in some conditions be genuinely described as rampant, though it will present problems when culture is at fault. It abhors wet conditions and seems to enjoy a warm, sunny position. As houseplants go, this dead nettle is unusual in that it produces orange-coloured flowers fairly freely. Alas, they are in no way an attraction, and they should be removed while still in bud on account of their abominable odour. Cuttings are little trouble to root, so it is better to propagate a few fresh young plants periodically and to dispose of the older ones when the new have rooted.

Senecio macroglossus variegatus
German ivy or Cape ivy

Deceptive, in that it is frequently mistaken for an ivy, *Senecio macroglossus variegatus* is recognised as something different when one touches the thick, fleshy leaves. The shape of the leaf is more or less triangular, and the plant is a natural climber, twining itself around any convenient support. It is comparatively easy to please if given a light position and if the watering-can is used sparingly. Be particularly careful not to water freely during the winter months. The orange-coloured daisy flowers are attractive, but rather inconspicuous against the cream and green background of the foliage.

Euphorbiaceae

Spurge family

The members of the *Euphorbiaceae*, the spurge family, occur as both garden and houseplants and include an important genus of succulents. The brightly coloured Christmas flower, the poinsettia, is a well-known example, although it has a very different appearance from the plant listed here.

Ricinus communis
Castor oil plant

With leaves similar in shape to *Fatsia japonica* (with which it shares the common name of castor oil plant) *Ricinus communis* is an annual plant grown from seed that will reach some four to six feet in height, depending on treatment. To improve germination the seed should be soaked in warm water for several hours before sowing. Sow seed in the spring in peaty compost and pot on as necessary – the larger the eventual pot the larger (usually) the

Ricinus communis

plant. Reddish, palmate leaves are carried on upright stems, and make the ricinus an attractive plant either for indoors or as a centre piece in the summer flower border.

Liliaceae

Lily family
The *Liliaceae* or lily family is known to everybody and, like many other plant families, it includes subjects which bear little superficial resemblance to each other. If a sansevieria plant is placed next to a hyacinth in flower, the uninitiated would find it difficult to believe that they are botanically related. However, see *Sansevieria trifasciata laurentii* in flower in mid-summer and the similarity is immediately made clear. The pale green, faintly scented flowers of this sansevieria are frequently looked upon as something of a phenomenon, but they are, in fact, quite freely produced on mature plants. Occasionally the small sansevieria will also oblige with a flower and the owner may with some justification feel that his plant deserves more than a passing glance.

Aspidistra lurida
Cast iron plant
The cast iron plant, *Aspidistra lurida*, is the toughie to outlast all toughies, and there is a keen desire by many to see the return of the aspidistra to the nurseryman's list. Sad to say, the aspidistra, besides being durable, is also lamentably slow-growing when compared to the more modern houseplant. The cost of growing them today would be prohibitive and beyond the purse of most would-be purchasers.

When I asked an old gardener how he cared for his 60-year-old cast iron plant that was growing in good health, he supplied the following rather surprising answer: 'Every springtime I knock it out of its pot, remove about one-third of the soil (roots and all) from the lower part of the root ball. Then I put a crock over the hole in the bottom of the pot, add an equivalent amount of soil to that which was removed from the root ball, and place the plant on top of it. After watering in, the plant never looks back'. Drastic, but effective.

Aspidistra lurida

Chlorophytum capense variegatum
Spider plant
This is another favourite houseplant that can be propagated without difficulty. Grass-like in appearance, chlorophytums produce plantlets on long stalks that can be rooted in ordinary soil by pegging them down in much the same way as one would layer a strawberry runner. Plants are sometimes reluctant to produce these little ones but it has been my experience that, when large enough, all chlorophytums produce young plantlets, and very fine they are when seen trailing from a hanging basket. For success, keep them well watered, well fed, and pot them on into slightly larger containers annually in the spring. Other than that, all they ask for is a light position and a moderate temperature. Browning of the leaf tips presents a minor problem, and is usually caused when plants are inadequately fed or are in need of potting on.

Sansevieria trifasciata laurentii
Mother-in-law's tongue
This plant seems to thrive on neglect, and is decidedly happier when the soil is very much on the dry side, particularly in winter. Cold

or wet conditions or a combination of the two are the worst enemies of this plant, but it will thrive in warm, sunny situations.

When purchasing, it is wise to select plants that have young shoots growing up at the side of the pot; one can then be reasonably sure that they are well-established.

As the rhizomes increase in both size and number they will break the pot in which they are growing, be it clay or plastic, and this is a positive sign that the plant is in need of fresh soil around the roots. Use John Innes No. 2 potting compost or a soilless potting compost and pot firmly. As older plants tend to become top-heavy it is wise to use heavier clay pots rather than plastic pots.

Marantaceae

Maranta family
It would be bold and foolish of me to include the entire maranta tribe – members of the *Marantaceae* – in this easily-grown section, but there are two that seem to qualify: *Maranta leuconeura kerchoveana* and *M. leuconeura erythrophylla*.

Maranta leuconeura kerchoveana
Rabbit's tracks or prayer plant
On reading the above heading one cannot help but feel that common names are, in their way, something of a blessing. For good measure this plant has two: rabbit's tracks, which it gets from the smudged brown spots on the attractive green leaf, and prayer plant. The reason for the second name is not obvious until the leaves are seen to fold up together like hands in prayer as darkness descends. This is a somewhat eerie sight when first seen by torchlight in a darkened greenhouse; leaves that were perfectly flat during the day having folded together showing only their reverse sides. One gets the feeling that every movement one makes is being watched!

Maranta leuconeura erythrophylla
Herringbone plant
Maranta leuconeura erythrophylla does, fortunately, have a common name, herringbone plant, which is a less tongue-twisting alternative for the layman. Understandably enough, this plant is also sold as *Maranta tricolor*. It is a particularly exciting plant that has come on the scene comparatively recently. At first sight the predominantly brown leaves, with quite fantastic stripes and patterns running through them, suggest a delicate stove (very warm greenhouse) type of plant. Limited experience has shown that it propagates

Maranta leuconeura kerchoveana. Inset shows leaf detail of M.l. erythrophylla

readily, and is more durable than almost any other plant in the entire family. However, do not run away with the idea that it is a tradescantia type of plant; it will require a minimum temperature of at least 18°C (65°F) and careful watering for success. When potting marantas, the addition of extra leafmould or peat to recommended composts is essential, and it should be firmed lightly. Exposure to strong, direct sunlight for any length of time should avoided, as it will quickly result in the leaves losing their colour and the plant taking on a generally hard appearance.

Moraceae

Fig family
The members of the *Moraceae* – it is a large family containing 55 genera – are mostly native to the tropics. In this family I am concerned only with the genus *Ficus* (the figs), a collection of plants of considerable importance to the houseplant enthusiast.

Ficus elastica robusta
Rubber plant
The rubber plant, *Ficus elastica robusta*, has, over the years, become the epitome of a houseplant. It would be virtually impossible to answer here all the questions that are asked about rubber plants, unless many other houseplants were to be excluded from the chapter. Also, since so many different species of ficus are cultivated in the home, I have decided to give general information on ficus culture rather than a catalogue of ficus names with specific cultural instructions.

Of all the questions that are asked, the most frequent is, without doubt, the one concerning loss of leaves. When plants lose their lower leaves it is, in most cases, due to overwatering, although it is quite natural for older plants to shed leaves as they increase in height. During the winter months water should be given sparingly as the plants are dormant and, therefore, need much less moisture. Rapid defoliation suggests other possible causes such as: overfeeding; insecticides used incorrectly; the use of harmful oil-based leaf-cleaning agents applied too frequently or at excessive strength; or coal gas fumes.

Considerable harm is also done by potting plants at the wrong time of the year, or when, in fact, potting is unnecessary. The layman is frequently misled into feeling that the obvious answer to the appearance of yellow lower leaves is to purchase a larger pot and transfer his ailing plant to it. Potting on (in effect, removing the plant from one pot and putting it into a pot one size larger) and disturbing roots that are probably damaged anyway, is a positive way of writing the plant's death warrant. Sick plants should be carefully nursed back to health by placing them in a draught-free corner where an even temperature of about 18°C (65°F) can be maintained. Above all, water must be given sparingly to give new roots an opportunity to get on the move.

Some ficus owners are plagued by their plants losing leaves, while others are casting worried glances at the top of the plant as it makes its way inexorably towards the ceiling. It was at one time a standing joke to suggest cutting a hole in the ceiling so that the plant could also be admired in the bedroom above!

For plants that are getting too tall and running out of head-room, one of three solutions is suggested. First, ask your nurseryman if he will be prepared to accept it in exchange for a smaller one, with suitable cash adjustment, naturally. Secondly, consider lopping off the top of the plant – probably a more practical suggestion. Do this with sharp secateurs; cut straight through the main stem about 1 in above a leaf joint at the height you wish your plant to be. The cut will exude latex that will dry up in time or it may be sealed by rubbing it over with a little moist clay soil or ordinary compost. The plant will subsequently produce four or five new shoots from the topmost leaf joints, so giving it the appearance of a standard specimen, like a standard rose or fuchsia.

The third suggestion is for the more adventurous, and involves an operation known as air-layering, see page 158. The foregoing information applies to healthy rubber plants, and one should not be too optimistic when treating ailing plants in this way.

Indoors, the rubber plant has a growing season that extends, more or less, from March through to October, during which time it will put on an average of one leaf per month – many more where conditions are favourable. However, some plants will go through the entire summer and develop no new leaves at all, and for no apparent reason. Occasionally, if the plant suffers a setback it will stop growing for a time; until, in fact, conditions are again to its liking. At these times it is particularly important to ensure that the winter watering procedure is practised, that is, giving water only when it is obviously required.

Temperature is quite important if plants are to develop leaves of normal size; over 18°C (65°F) the leaves will be larger than normal and inclined to droop, under 7°C (45°F) much smaller leaves will result. Plants that have been subjected to widely fluctuating temperatures will show this by producing large or small leaves, depending upon the temperature prevailing at the time these leaves were about to open.

Piperaceae

Pepper family
This family contains a group of plants known as peperomias. There are many different species and varieties the majority of which are compact and low growing. Those with variegated leaves need ample light in order to retain their attractive colouring while those with darker leaves become hard in appearance when exposed to excessive sunlight.

The best-known peperomias
Best known of the peperomias are *Peperomia magnoliaefolia*, with fleshy leaves, cream and green in colour; *P. hederaefolia*, with metallic grey leaves; and the attractive dark green, crinkle-leaved species, *P. caperata*. The last two are not difficult to propagate if this is done by leaf cuttings in the manner of saintpaulias (African violets).

Three types of peperomia

With the variegated sorts it is necessary to take a cutting with part of the stem attached to the leaf if a variegated plant is to result from the propagation. Cuttings prepared from leaves only will result in green growth. Yet the leaves of *P. sandersii*, with dark stripes of green on the grey background, can be propagated by cutting the leaf into sections, and the resultant growth is invariably identical to the parent leaf in both colour and pattern.

Peperomia rotundifolia is the most recent to be tried as a houseplant. It has plain green, rather uninteresting leaves, but it has an advantage over most indoor plants in that it regularly produces its clean, white flowers. When the flowers fade, cut back to a sound pair of leaves, so that fresh growth may be encouraged.

Proteaceae

Protea family
The *Proteaceae* or protea family is a large group of plants containing many large shrubs, which were particularly popular over 100 years ago when large conservatories were fashionable and could provide the plants with the protection that most of them require.

Grevillea robusta
Australian wattle or silk oak
Here again we have two common names for the same plant – the Australian wattle and the silk oak. It is a fast-growing green plant, that quickly adapts itself to most reasonable growing conditions. It is easily reared from

seed, and besides being an attractive indoor plant it plays an important part as the centre-piece of bedding schemes in many public parks during the summer months.

Rapid growth is a drawback in some respects, as grevilleas will outgrow their headroom in a matter of two or three years, if conditions are to their liking. Ideally, by the time it reaches the ceiling the keen houseplant grower should have a younger plant growing on, ready to take the place of the larger one. It is not everyone who has the heart to destroy over-grown, healthy plants, so finding a suitable home for the monster becomes a problem. The garage showroom, or the hotel manager will often take these off your hands and give them a home where overhead space is improved by the presence of the silk oak.

Saxifragaceae

Saxifrage family
The plants of this family are well known to everyone. The production of new plants from small plantlets is a characteristic feature and is clearly shown in the houseplant members of the family.

Saxifraga sarmentosa
Mother of thousands
Saxifraga sarmentosa, an attractive trailing plant with small pink and white flowers, makes rapid growth, and ease of propagation ensures that it will retain its popularity. Mother of thousands, as it is called, is seen to best advantage when placed in a pot or small orchid-type slatted-wood basket and suspended from the window lintel. Small plantlets snipped from the parent plant establish themselves readily.

Tolmiea menziesii
Pick-a-back plant
Described as a hardy perennial herb, *Tolmiea menziesii* is also a fine indoor plant that is very much neglected in this respect. Outdoors the foliage will die back in winter, indoors it will remain evergreen.

This is a particularly easy plant to care for, and has the amusing common name of pick-a-back plant, which it gets from the way young plantlets are formed and carried 'on the back' of older leaves. These young plantlets root with ease in ordinary compost if they are inserted with the parent leaf still attached.

Avoid overwatering, especially during the winter months, but keep moist and well-fed at other times once plants have become well-established.

Grevillea robusta

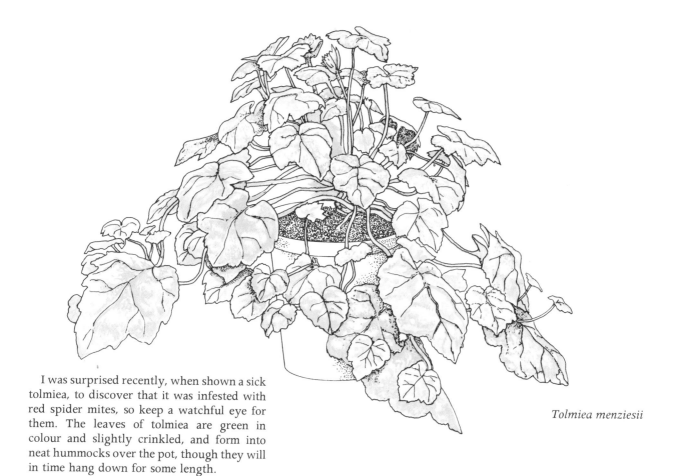

Tolmiea menziesii

I was surprised recently, when shown a sick tolmiea, to discover that it was infested with red spider mites, so keep a watchful eye for them. The leaves of tolmiea are green in colour and slightly crinkled, and form into neat hummocks over the pot, though they will in time hang down for some length.

Urticaceae

Nettle family
Apart from the well known weeds the nettle family contains several good garden plants and two important genera of houseplants.

Pileas
Aluminium plant
The nettle family's two main contributions to the modern houseplant scene are the attractive variegated plants *Pilea cadierei* and *P. cadierei minima*. The latter is rapidly gaining in popularity over its larger-leaved forbear. These have aluminium-coloured leaves (hence the common name aluminium plant) and are comparatively easy to care for; only when the compost is well filled with roots are they inclined to become hard in appearance and less attractive. Like tradescantias, they are simple to propagate, so it should be the rule to raise new plants from fresh cuttings periodically. Regular pinching out of the growing tips is necessary if growth is not to become leggy. Remember a small, bushy, 'well-furnished' plant is much more attractive than an ungainly, sprawling large one.

Pilea cadierei (**above**) *and Pilea Moon Valley* (**below**)

Pilea mollis
Pilea Moon Valley

Pilea mollis is much better known by its common name of _P._ Moon Valley, and is one of our most attractive smaller foliage plants. These plants may be used to good effect as individuals on the windowsill, as part of a group planting, or may be seen at their best when several small plants are gathered together in a shallow dish. The rough texture of the leaves and their attractive golden-green colouring make these very attractive plants. They are not difficult to manage if given reasonable warmth and light. Occasional pinching out of the growing tips will keep plants compact and bushy.

Coleus
Flame nettle

Coleus in their many brilliant colours are invariably a good purchase, as they are inexpensive and not in the least difficult to manage. Plants grown from seed are available in the spring and will usually require potting on into slightly larger containers soon after purchase. Use a fairly rich compost and pinch out the growing tip of the plant after it has been potted – this will encourage the plant to branch and form an attractive bushy shape.

Coleus, showing a variety of leaf markings

Select the best colours when purchasing young plants, or if you wish to grow the plants from seed, again select and retain only plants of better colouring. Plants of particular merit can be retained to grow on the following year, or new plants may be easily raised from seed sown in the spring. In time coleus tend to become untidy and overgrown, and it is then a good idea to propagate new plants from the topmost stem sections; pieces with three or four leaves attached will be about the right size.

Besides the run of the mill sorts that are raised from seed there are also many excellent named varieties available from nurserymen that have splendid colouring, and in some cases seem to have a superior habit of growth.

Vitaceae

Vine family

A characteristic of the vine family or _Vitaceae_ is that the majority of the members of the family are climbers and produce tendrils which help them to attach themselves to supports.

Cissus antarctica and Rhoicissus rhomboidea
Kangaroo vine and grape ivy

The two important contributions made by the vine family to present-day house plant displays are the kangaroo vine, _Cissus antarctica_, and the grape ivy, _Rhoicissus rhomboidea_. The first-mentioned is reasonably easy under most conditions, though it does not approve of hot, dry rooms, particularly if the compost in the pot is allowed to become too dry. Under these conditions, the leaves take on a crisp, dry appearance, and the plant does not recover very readily. Yet its close relative, the grape ivy (there is also the larger-leaved _Rhoicissus rhomboidea_ Jubilee) is probably the most durable of all indoor plants. Of climbing habit, it has naturally glossy leaves.

A few years ago an observant Danish nurseryman detected a variation in one of his plants – a piece with shallow-indentations along the margin of the leaf. The rogue piece was nursed along with more than a little care, and we now have a new variety freely available called _Rhoicissus ellendanica_, which is a combination of the nurseryman's wife's name, Ellen and danica for Denmark.

Although the indentations distinguish it from the grape ivy, the leaves have the same attractive glossy appearance of the parent, and it is equally easy to care for which means that it is one of the plants best suited to indoor growing.

CHAPTER 5
Distinctive houseplants

When gathering together a collection of plants it is wise to include a few that are out of the ordinary, be it for their flowers, leaf colour, or simply because they have an unusual shape.

Because of their habit of growth or their colouring many plants can claim to be distinctive, some easy to care for while others will prove more testing. Whatever their merits in respect of culture, there is little doubt that the inclusion of a selection of distinctive plants will enhance the appearance and prove more interesting in almost every collection of indoor plants. Some of the plant varieties mentioned will in all probability prove difficult to acquire, but obtaining material is all part of the challenge when it comes to growing more distinctive plants.

Acorus gramineus variegatus
Easy
Of the grassy-foliaged plants available, the golden-leaved acorus is one of the best, being compact, colourful and easy to grow. With almost any other houseplant it would be fatal if it were allowed to stand in water for any length of time, but the acorus is rarely too wet, and will often do better if the pot is partly submerged in water. It is a particularly fine plant for a bottle garden.

Aglaonema
Moderately difficult
In the past few months I have been agreeably surprised at the way in which a plant of *Aglaonema pseudo-bracteatum* has tolerated indifferent treatment and the smoky atmosphere of a club bar. In its favour, no doubt, is the constant minimum temperature of 17°C (63°F) that is maintained for 24 hours a day. Aglaonemas are difficult to purchase, but there seems to be much interest in the new variety Silver Queen which is short and compact with silver-grey leaves and which is likely to become more easily available in time.

Mealy bug is a troublesome pest that is difficult to eradicate and it will attack the roots as well as the leaves of this plant. A thorough drenching with malathion insecticide diluted according to the manufacturer's instructions is effective if the bug is detected in time.

Araucaria excelsa
Norfolk Island pine. Easy
Araucaria excelsa, popular in the past, is slowly coming back into favour as a decorative houseplant. In common with many of the Victorian potted plants, it is slow growing and therefore, by definition, costly. In a cool room, where the temperature need not exceed 10°C (50°F), its tiered green leaves seldom fail to please. Water moderately, as the leaves quickly lose their crisp appearance if the compost is permanently wet; likewise, leaves are spoilt if the temperature is excessive. It is usual for new plants to be raised from seed, but this is a slow business. Sow seed in John Innes No. 1 potting compost or a soilless seed compost in February or March.

Begonia
Moderately easy
The rex types of begonias, with their intricate and colourful leaf patterns, are the best known. For indoor use, I find that some varieties of *Begonia rex* are better than others and, in particular, those with smaller leaves are easier to care for. After a time plants become unsightly when the rhizomatous growth extends beyond the edge of the pot, and lower leaves are lost in the process. Although it presents considerable difficulties, I have known enthusiasts succeed when attempting to root leaf cuttings in pans of moist peat on a window sill (for further details see page 162).

Besides the rex types there are many other equally interesting and attractive fibrous-rooted begonias, and one finds it difficult to understand why these delightful plants are not more popular. These range from the tiny

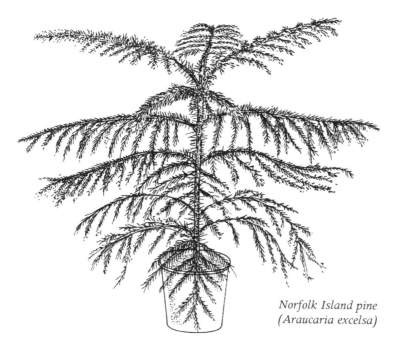

Norfolk Island pine (Araucaria excelsa)

light and dark green leaves of *B. boweri*, which develops into tight hummocks of overlapping leaves. Also among the smaller leaved sorts there is the slightly larger plant, *B. Cleopatra*, with bronzed foliage and typically lopsided begonia-shaped leaves. Of upright habit and growing to roughly six feet there is *B. maculata* with speckled grey-green colouring. All of these produce flowers, but they are insignificant when compared to the foliage.

Slightly more difficult to propagate than the *B. rex* varieties, *B. masoniana* (known as iron cross) is, however, a superior plant, both in respect of durability and usefulness. With its distinctive iron cross marking in the centre of each leaf, it is particularly easy to use in small bowl arrangements, and equally useful for blending with other plants in larger displays.

Caladium
Difficult

These aroids, available in many colours, have the most delicate foliage of all indoor plants. Indeed, the leaves of the most popular kind, *Caladium* Candidum, are almost transparent, yet it is one of the easiest to care for indoors. Last year I tried one for the first time, and felt I had had full value when it lasted for four-and-a-half months in an unheated room.

Corms are started into growth in warm peat beds in the greenhouse in the early part of the year, and the plants are on sale from the end of April. When the leaves die back naturally in the autumn one should be able, in theory, to allow the compost to dry before storing the corm in a minimum temperature of 16°C (60°F) until February, when the compost is gradually given more water to encourage fresh

growth. This I have done, and I await results but am not too hopeful, knowing that it can be difficult to overwinter caladiums even in a greenhouse where the conditions are almost ideal.

My plant responded to a watering programme that allowed the soil to dry a little between bouts with the watering-can. When a plant has been purchased, it is advisable to support the larger leaves with thin canes, as they become top heavy and the petioles bend very easily, restricting the flow of sap to the leaves and causing them to die.

Calathea
Difficult

Many calatheas are difficult indoors, and some downright impossible. Probably the easiest is *Calathea louisae*, which has less colourful leaves than many of the others. *C. insignis* and *C. ornata* Sanderiana are both very striking plants that will catch the eye in any collection. These, however, should be treated as being expendable and should not be expected to live for more than a year or two at the most. Calatheas will not tolerate direct sunlight at any cost; and warm, humid conditions must be the aim when caring for them.

Comparatively slow growth and difficulty of culture tends to make calatheas costly and scarce.

Calathea louisae

Citrus mitis

Calamondin orange. Moderately easy
Citrus mitis is a winner all the way, but it can be somewhat aggravating to see yellow, chlorotic leaves develop – as they often do – when the correct cultural needs of the plant have been supplied to the letter. The Calamondin orange, as it is commonly called, is short and compact, without the spines normally associated with citrus plants. It has the considerable advantage over *C. sinensis*, the more common species, of bearing fruit on comparatively small plants.

Citrus mitis

In America these dwarf oranges are extremely popular, and to encourage sales the story goes that no cocktail bar is complete without its real live orange tree from which oranges can be plucked and used for flavouring. Having seen both, it would seem that the American product is very much better than our home-reared plants; success across the Atlantic owing much to the abundant sunshine available in California for ripening one-year-old wood that will bear fruit the following year. Providing the plants with the maximum amount of sunshine during the summer months, when they can be put outside, is one way of encouraging them to flower and fruit. Guard against over-watering, as the weak root system quickly dies in wet conditions. Cuttings root with little difficulty, and these will sometimes fruit as little as 12 months from potting. The fruits resemble tangerine oranges and peel in much the same way, but are somewhat bitter.

Codiaeum

Croton. Difficult
There seems to be no limit to the range and variety of colours to be found in codiaeum (croton) leaves, and these colours will improve considerably if the plants are exposed to the maximum amount of light available. In common with most plants of ornamental appearance, the codiaeum is a stove (very warm greenhouse) subject, so it must have an adequate temperature – 18°C (65°F) or more. Both low temperatures and dry conditions will result in leaf drop and the soil need only be very dry on one occasion for leaves to fall a week or two later.

Keep feeding codiaeums while they are actively growing, and pot them on annually into slightly larger containers; John Innes No. 2 potting compost, well firmed, is the growing mixture to use. Red spider mite is a troublesome pest and a watchful eye (assisted by a magnifying glass) should be kept on the underside of leaves for signs of its presence.

Codiaeum reidii is recognised by keen plantsmen as one of the finest pot plants at present in cultivation. Mature specimens, growing in ideal greenhouse conditions, may have leaves as much as 18 in long and 9 in across. These leaves are beautifully patterned and are predominantly orange-pink in colour. Not easy to grow indoors, it will, however, be well worth purchasing, if only to provide a spring and summer display.

The variety Mrs Iceton has smaller leaves almost like a rainbow in their range of colour. It requires maximum light for best results. Much confusion exists over the proper naming of codiaeums and this plant is no exception, there being two other names to my knowledge – Annie Bier and Volcano. When it is seen almost erupting into colour, one realises that the last-mentioned name is not inappropriate. A point in favour of Mrs Iceton, not shared by many codiaeums, is the way in which foliage that has almost completely reverted to green will regain its exotic colouring as soon as the drab days of winter are left behind.

With bright yellow colouring, C. Eugene Drapps, will in ideal conditions develop into a giant some 8 ft in height to become a truly distinctive plant. Although not often sold by varietal name it is easily detected in the retailer's collection by its very colourful appearance. Combining elegance with distinction, *C. warrenii* has leaves little more than an inch wide and some twelve inches in length, and forms into a neat clump if the growing points are periodically removed.

Possibly the most popular of all codiaeums,

Codiaeum Mrs Iceton

C. holuffiana, with yellow to orange colouring, is generally sold in very large quantities during the summer months.

Dieffenbachia

Dumb cane. Moderately difficult

All of these may safely be described as delicate plants that will require a minimum temperature of not less than 18°C (65°F), both by day and night. In the greenhouse, some varieties

Dieffenbachia picta exotica

attain a maximum height of about 5 ft by which time they will have lost many of their lower leaves and will be producing young plants at soil level from the base of the parent stem.

When the plant is no longer attractive, the main stem can be cut back almost to soil level, and the top portion may be propagated as a very large cutting; but unless conditions are good, one should not be too optimistic about the results. The bare stem of the plant can be cut up into pieces about 4 in in length, each with a node or joint, and laid on their sides partly buried in fresh peat. Keep the peat at about 18°C (65°F); it is surprising the way in which some of these tough old stumps will develop into new plants.

Dieffenbachia has the unusual common name of dumb cane, which it gets from the fact that speech becomes difficult for a day or two should one inadvertently get the sap on one's tongue. However, since dieffenbachias smell so abominably when cut, such an event is most unlikely.

One of my personal favourites among the dieffenbachia tribe is *D. oerstedii*, which has dark green, almost black, leaves of roughly oval shape with a striking mid-rib, ivory white in colour, that runs the entire length of the leaf. *Dieffenbachia bauseii* is another fine plant with an almost white stem and dark, speckled, light green leaves – a plant guaranteed to improve any collection. With cream and green leaves *D. picta* is probably a little easier to acquire, while its improved form, *D. picta* Superba, with brighter cream colouring will require that little extra care and attention if it is to succeed.

Since the introduction of *Dieffenbachia amoena* from America about fifteen years ago it has gained many admirers. The bold, dark green leaves require space in which to spread so spacious surroundings are the answer. Water should be given with care, as excessive moisture will result in the main stem splitting at the base and eventually rotting. *D. arvida exotica* has been with us about the same length of time as *D. amoena* and is, if anything, more popular. Being more compact and slower growing than the latter it is much better suited to average room conditions.

Foliage plants are becoming increasingly popular for use in planted bowls, and florists frequently include one or two exotic plants, such as *D. exotica*, in order to catch the customer's eye. As a result, I am often asked how such arrangements should be cared for – a problem indeed. I find, however, that it is invariably better to place the container in a room temperature that will suit the more delicate subjects. While the majority of easier plants will tolerate the higher temperatures it will be found that the delicate plant will quickly succumb in colder conditions. In respect of watering, one should always aim at the happy medium, at all costs avoiding overwatering as many of these bowls have no drainage so an excess of water just collects in the bottom of the container.

Dizygotheca elegantissima
Difficult

Belonging to the same family as the hederas, or ivies, *Dizygotheca elegantissima* is, however, a much more trying plant to care for, wet and cold conditions reducing it to a bare stalk in a

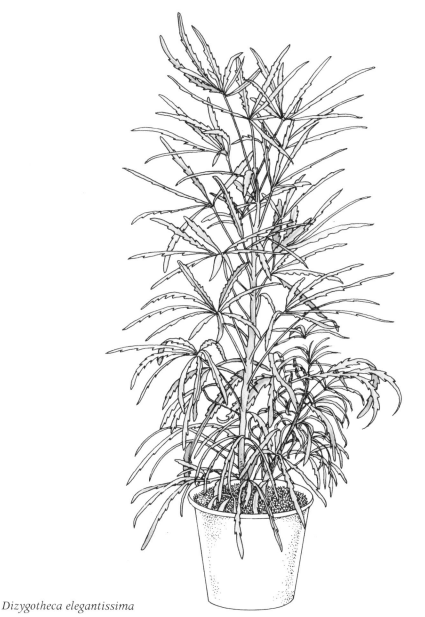

Dizygotheca elegantissima

very short space of time. A temperature of 18°C (65°F) is required for successful cultivation, the soil being kept moist, but never saturated. Surprisingly enough it adapts itself very well to the modern technique of capillary watering. Plastic pots are used when plants are watered in this way as the thin base permits the compost in the pot and the sand to come into direct contact.

Mature plants of eight years or more in age lose much of their fine-leaved, elegant appearance as they develop into small trees, the leaves becoming much coarser and larger in the process. There is little fear of having them push the roof off indoors though, as growth becomes much slower, and even an expert would have difficulty in keeping plants for more than a few years.

Dracaena
Easy and difficult

Several species of dracaena are available and the best known is probably *Dracaena terminalis*, a somewhat difficult plant which is prone to brown leaf tips as a result of root failure. A light position is preferred, and it is especially important that soft water should be given in preference to hard tap water. The stiff red leaves are much prized by the enthusiastic flower arranger, but to me it seems almost criminal to strip leaves off this aristocrat among plants for such a purpose.

Dracaena sanderiana has grey and white narrow leaves on slender stems, and presents something of a problem in respect of culture. Excessively wet compost allied to low temperatures will almost certainly result in browning of the leaf tips. Although plants with single stems may appear unimpressive, I find that when planted in groups of a dozen or more they are indispensible for display work. Should one own a number of these plants it will be found that a much more pleasing effect can be achieved by potting several together; three plants to a 5 in pot is about right. Overgrown plants can be cut back and will develop new shoots from the old stem, as well as from soil level.

A dracaena of distinctive appearance is *D. godseffiana* Florida Beauty, a variety with oval leaves borne close together on low growing stems and heavily spotted with cream.

A distinctive plant of easy culture, *D. volckaertii*, has narrow, dark green leaves borne on a slender stem, making it an excellent plant as a background subject in a group of plants. Keep the soil on the dry side and offer a reasonably light location with a temperature in the region of 16°C to 18°C (60° to 65°F).

Much shorter and more compact, with

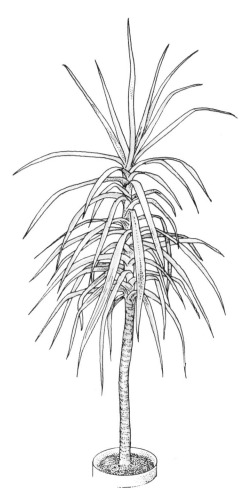

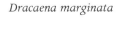

Dracaena marginata

Ficus elastica tricolor is an attractive plant, similar to the ordinary rubber plant, but with variegated leaves of pink, cream and green. When first introduced it was hailed as being a plant of good temperament, needing little more care than the green rubber plant. Browning of leaf margins tends to be a problem and is usually associated with wet, cold conditions. It does, however, have the remarkable capacity of growing away clean and strong for a second time when the stems have been cut to stumps of little more than 3 or 4 in in height. So, do not completely despair when plants lose their leaves and are no longer attractive – instead, try cutting them back. Cut back plants will, of course, require only the bare minimum amount of water until such time as new leaves are produced.

Another variegated ficus is *F.* Zulu Shield, which has brightly variegated leaves that are identical in shape to those of the common rubber plant. My personal experience of this plant suggests that it has many fine qualities, not least among them the plant's ability to grow at a reasonable pace if provided with good light (not direct sunlight) and watering that ensures that the soil does not remain wet

leaves of attractive dull red colouring, *D. Redege* will have to be maintained at the higher temperature recommended above if it is to do well. This one is excellent for mixed plantings in tubs or even the larger plant cases.

One of the toughest of the dracaenas, *D. marginata*, has a relative in *D. marginata tricolor*, which has a soft creamy-pink colouring that is most attractive. However, it is a much more difficult plant to care for and will need a temperature in the region of 18°C (65°F) and careful watering that errs on the dry side.

Ficus
Rubber plant. Easy and difficult
Besides the ordinary rubber plant, *Ficus elastica robusta*, (see page 61) there are many other ficus plants available, some easy to care for, others not so easy. At the extreme ends of the scale, in respect of size, there is the stately fiddle-leaved fig. *F. lyrata*, and the creeping *F. radicans variegata*, neither of which is easy to grow. Given ideal conditions, *F. lyrata* reaches tree-like proportions in time, and will tolerate quite severe pruning when established.

Ficus elastica tricolor

for long periods. Less water and feeding are necessary in winter.

Ficus Black Prince has, as the name suggests, very much darker leaves than any of the other rubber plants. Care is very much the same, also the habit of growth, but if anything the plant is a little more temperamental than the other ficuses.

Fittonia
Difficult

Fittonia argyroneura and *F. verschaffeltii* have similar habits of growth, but are easily distinguishable, the first having silvered leaves and the latter leaves which are reddish brown in colour. Both are suitable bottle garden plants and should be given a minimum temperature of at least 18°C (65°F), and a certain amount of humidity. Water should be given in moderation; indeed, *F. argyroneura* has quite astonishing powers of recovery after the compost has become really bone-dry. Leaves suffering from drought will collapse to the point when they will appear to be quite shrivelled and lifeless; yet, after watering, they soon become firm again.

The miniature form of the silver fittonia, *F.a.* Nana, is a recent development. The markings on the leaves are equally attractive but it seems much easier to care for than its parent form. Peaty compost is essential, as is the need for shade and careful watering.

Heptapleurum
Easy

One of the most exciting houseplants to appear recently is *Heptapleurum arboricola*, and its similar relatives *H.* Hong Kong and *H.* Geisha Girl. Tall, erect stems carry palmate leaves that are not dissimilar to its relation, schefflera, which give the plant a most elegant appearance. Grow in light shade at a temperature of around 18°C (65°F) and water and feed in moderation. Plants can be pruned to shape at any time, and are often seen at their best with branching green stems rather than slender single stemmed specimens.

Isolepis gracilis
Easy

Isolepis gracilis (syn. *Scirpus cernuus*) is an adaptable plant. Trouble free, it puts up with wide variations in temperature, and asks for little more than sufficient water to keep the soil moist, and occasional feeding with liquid fertiliser. It is easily propagated by dividing the roots and potting them up individually in any reasonable compost. Although it would appear to be a member of the grass family, it is in fact a miniature bulrush.

Overleaf Ferns grow well when grouped together and, as long as there is no draught, can tolerate the shady conditions of a fireplace. The atmosphere around them must never be allowed to dry out so frequent spraying with a hand mister is important. The variety of leaf shapes and textures available makes them fascinating to collect.

1 *Asparagus plumosus*
2 *Nephrolepis exaltata bostoniensis*
3 *Adiantum cuneatum*
4 *Platycerium alcicorne*
5 *Asplenium nidus avis*
6 A group of small ferns
7 *Pteris ensiformis*

Fittonia verschaffeltii

Far left *Maranta picturata*

Left *Philodendron melanochrysum*

Maranta picturata
Difficult

Maranta picturata is a difficult plant to grow, and not easy to obtain, but it is a particular favourite of mine – hence my reason for including it. The leaves are light grey, compactly arranged with dark green margins and maroon undersides; they seldom fail to attract attention. A shaded position, with a temperature of 18°C (65°F) and high humidity, will provide ideal growing conditions. Plants are increased by means of cuttings, which are prepared from pieces of growth about 4 in in length with two or three leaves attached. Insert them in 3-in pots of moist peat. They may also be increased by division in the early part of the year and, if one is lucky enough, plants will occasionally have a colony of self-set seedlings around them. However, it must be confessed that a heated greenhouse, with plants standing on a moist peat bed, is almost essential for the latter to take place. As a general guide, if delicate plants require a growing temperature of about 18°C (65°F) one may safely assume that at least 3°C (5°F) more heat will be needed when propagating new plants.

Persea gratissima
Avocado pear. Easy

You buy the pear, plant the stone, and in time you will have the satisfaction of saying that you did it all yourself. Unfortunately, these plants grow rapidly indoors and the larger leaves tend to droop eventually. To keep the plant reasonably compact the leading shoots should be pinched out occasionally. In average room conditions the avocado pear will soon outgrow its allotted space, and the owner is then faced with the problem of what is to be done with it – few of us have the heart to put a healthy plant in the dustbin. Sad to say, I cannot help here, as it often requires a little diplomacy and a chat with the local garage proprietor who may be prepared to accept it for his showroom. At all costs, keep away from your florist and nurseryman, as they have, no doubt, had to say 'No' in the past when asked to provide a home for overgrown avocado pears.

Planting the stone is a simple operation; for details see page 163.

Philodendron melanochrysum
Moderately difficult

The heart-shaped leaves with brown velvet colouring make this plant well worth trying, even though it has the reputation of being difficult. A temperature in the region of 18°C (65°F) and humid conditions are both important.

It is probably an ambitious thought for the indoor plantsman, but hanging baskets filled with these philodendrons can look very striking, and might be worth trying. I well remember the mystified observers in Paris a few years ago, at an international flower show which I attended, when they saw a fine basketful of *Philodendron melanochrysum* twist first one way then the other with no visible means of support, or propulsion. They were not to know that nylon fishing line supported the basket, and the circulating warm air in the building was keeping it on the move. It is odd that, at flower shows, the slightest movement, be it only a drip of water in a pool, will attract more attention than the most exotic plant life in the vicinity!

Scindapsus aureus
Money plant or devil's ivy. Moderately difficult

I often wonder if plants can change or adapt their needs in respect of general care: the reason for asking is that plants of *Scindapsus aureus* were at one time among the more delicate of indoor subjects, yet I now see them growing in all sorts of unlikely places with little discernible effort. However, a steady temperature in the region of 16°C to 18°C (60° to 65°F) is important, and plants should be well watered, although allowed to dry a little before repeating. The same applies for *S. Marble Queen*, but one would not expect an especially good response from this more temperamental plant.

Sparmannia africana
Indoor lime or African windflower. Easy

Sparmannia africana has two common names, the indoor lime, which it gets from the appearance of the cool, green foliage, and the African windflower, because of the way in which the flowers open outwards at the slightest breath of wind.

In ideal conditions it will quickly outgrow its welcome, but one can quite severely prune the branches to shape at almost any time. It is not often grown commercially, as demand is very limited, and growth in greenhouse conditions is frequently rampant enough to become an embarrassment to the commercial grower. A fine plant for a cool, light room, it will give little trouble if regular feeding and annual potting on are not neglected. In common with many of the easier plants, it can be increased readily from cuttings, so it is advisable to start new plants every few years.

Temperature around 16°C (60°F) will suit these, and they should be watered more freely during summer than winter, but never allowed to dry out. Large pale green leaves are a constant attraction, with interesting flowers that appear in summer being an added bonus.

Sparmannia africana

Right Dracaena, calathea and dieffenbachia are all plants grown for their distinctive foliage

Opposite page
Top *Araucaria excelsa*
Bottom left A large-leafed pink caladium
Bottom right One of the colourful varieties of codiaeum

Palms

In their many forms, palms have been among the most popular of potted plants for a century or more, and there does not appear to be any sort of decline in spite of the high cost of cultivation and the subsequent high purchase price.

Howeia forsteriana
Parlour palm. Easy
Queen of the palms as far as indoor use is concerned is *Howeia forsteriana* (much more popularly known as *Kentia forsteriana*) which has segmented leaves held high on stout stems. As individual, or specimen plants for any form of decoration they are unsurpassed, and with reasonable care will continue in fine condition for many years.

Reasonable care entails the maintenance of a minimum temperature of around 18°C (65°F), a light but not sunny location and watering that is done thoroughly, but not to excess. The safest method of watering is to fill the pot with water and allow the surplus to drain away through the bottom of the pot – a few insignificant dribbles indicates that not enough water has been given. It is then essential to allow the soil to dry a little before repeating the watering exercise. Feed estab-lished plants at regular intervals while new leaves are being produced with a weak solution of liquid fertiliser. When potting on use a mixture of peat and leafmould and pot with reasonable firmness. Spring and early summer are the best potting times.

The above advice applies to almost all the palm plants that one may purchase. It is also best to never clean the leaves with any form of chemical cleaner – spray the leaves with water frequently and occasionally wipe with a damp cloth to remove surface dust.

Besides *Howeia (Kentia) forsteriana* there is also the similar plant *H. belmoreana*, but the latter is a very much stronger growing plant that is only suitable for premises that can offer the necessary headroom. The leaves are also coarser in appearance.

Cocos weddelliana
Coconut palm. Easy
One of the smallest and most delicate of palms is *Cocos weddelliana* which is usually bought in pots that have no drainage holes in the bottom. In their early stages these plants do grow better for this treatment, but will do just as well later on if grown in more conventional containers. The foliage of this plant is very fine and delicate, which makes it a very useful plant for mixed displays.

Howeia forsteriana,
popularly known as Kentia

Chamaedorea elegans
also *Neanthe bella*. Easy

The palms seem to be beset with dull names, and in *Chamaedorea elegans* we have a plant that is much more popularly known as *Neanthe bella*. A very slow growing plant that will go on for many years if a careful eye is kept for the presence of red spider mite on the undersides of leaves.

Phoenix roebelenii

Phoenix
Moderately easy

Phoenix dactylifera takes many years to reach maturity, but presents the interesting prospect that it can be raised from a date stone that is subjected to a high temperature of not less than 21°C (70°F) while germinating. Another palm with similar appearance is *P. canariensis* which produces masses of roots and has vicious barbs along the midrib of the leaf. Of similar shape, but more delicate and much more attractive as a plant for a large room is *P. roebelinii*.

Chamaerops
Fan palm. Moderately easy

As the common name suggests the fan palms have leaves that fan out from the petiole, much as the fingers fan out from the palm of the hand. The most popular of these are *Chamaerops humilis* and *C. elegans* (which is more popularly known as *Trachycarpus fortunei*). Both of these require reasonable space if they are to be seen at their best.

Care of palms

Indoors, palms can be very unpredictable in respect of growing performance; in some situations they are difficult to manage, while at other times they are completely trouble free. For example, I know of one *Howeia belmoreana* growing in a 15-in pot that is well over eighty years of age. Why it does so well is a complete mystery as it has to suffer the somewhat harsh treatment every fourth year or so of having its roots severely pruned in order to restrict its top growth. It is virtually a very old and very majestic Bonsai plant – however, it should be added that it is growing within the confines of a heated greenhouse with expert care.

You are seldom likely to walk into a garden centre, and find packets of palm seeds in the racks being offered for sale. Banana and all sorts of other unlikely seeds are often on offer but not palm. The reason for this is that palm seed is almost permanently in short supply, and the small amount available is much in demand by the commercial grower the world over. However, should one be fortunate enough to come across a supply, the seed should be buried in a very porous compost mixture in a temperature of not less than 21°C (70°F). Germination will take six to eight weeks, often longer. One porous mixture that I recall using with a high success rate was very fine coke breeze that was kept well moistened, but because of its composition it could never become excessively wet and cause seed to deteriorate.

Ferns

I, personally, find plants endlessly fascinating and when I cast my eyes on some of the more delicate ferns (maidenhair, for example), both indoors and out, I find it difficult to believe that anything so delicate and beautiful can survive. Yet survive they do, and many of them are very tolerant of the often indifferent conditions that we offer them indoors. But there are the exceptions, and it would seem that the tender adiantum, or maidenhair, does present more than a few problems in the room where the atmosphere is excessively dry.

Above all else, it is essential that the ferns have a shaded location in which to grow, and that there should be plenty of moisture around them. This should not be construed as meaning that the compost in the pot should remain sopping wet. Ideally, the compost should be well drained and kept moist – a condition that lies between wet and dry. With ferns, I feel that it is important to place a collection of

continued on page 84

The
Bathroom

The humid atmosphere makes bathrooms excellent places in which to grow plants. Bathrooms tend to be cooler and often darker than the rest of the house so ferns such as *Asparagus plumosus*, *A. sprengeri* and adiantum **(below)** are ideal. The spider plant, *Chlorophytum comosum* **(right)** can withstand almost any conditions but this position in a jardinière in front of the windows shows off its graceful, arching leaves and stems to their best advantage. Other plants which will grow successfully in a bathroom are the moisture-loving philodendrons, particularly *Philodendron scandens* with its twisting stems and heart-shaped leaves, and also the many varieties of tradescantia.

Three delicate-leaved ferns: Pellaea rotundifolia (bottom left), Asparagus plumosus (bottom right) and Adiantum flabellulatum (behind)

plants together in a larger container that is filled with peat, moss or some other moisture-retaining material.

Excessive feeding of ferns is to my mind detrimental rather than beneficial, and I am firmly of the opinion that the vast majority of these plants are far better off with a regular foliar feed only.

Many of the smaller ferns (*Pellaea rotundifolia*, *Pteris argyraea*, *P. cretica*, and *P. ensiformis* Victoriae to name but a few) are excellent plants for use in bottle gardens.

Nephrolepis fern
Moderately easy

There are many variations of the nephrolepis fern, and almost all of them are among the royalty of the plant business; they have few peers. As an individual plant in a hanging basket or a large pot, they present a splendid sight with their bright green leaves radiating in all directions from the heart of the plant. In a small greenhouse that is heated to around 18°C (65°F), new plants can be easily propagated if the parent plant has its pot plunged in a bed of moist peat, and plantlets on the ends of long runners are allowed to root into the plunging medium.

When purchased, any ferns that appear too large for their pots should be potted on immediately using a very peaty potting mixture. This applies in particular to plants that are in smaller pots of around 3 in in diameter.

Asparagus sprengeri and A. plumosus
Asparagus fern. Moderately easy

With trailing sprays of greenery, *Asparagus sprengeri*, is a most prolific plant that will flourish given the cultural care mentioned earlier. Having more upright and rather more delicate foliage, *A. plumosus*, is a reliable plant that will go on for many years with comparatively little attention. Equally distinctive and quite different to these two is *A. meyeri* which develops stiff cylindrical sprays of greenery. (Although universally referred to as ferns these, in fact, belong to the lily family).

Asplenium nidus avis
Bird's nest fern. Moderately easy

This attractive plant produces smooth pale green leaves that radiate from the centre of the plant, so that it is similar in shape to a shuttle-cock. Generally it is a trying plant to grow indoors; an even temperature in the region of 18°C (65°F) is essential, also fairly high humidity.

Contrary to general advice, feeding with weak liquid fertiliser will preserve the pale green colouring of its leaves. When dark brown 'spider's legs' of roots begin to creep over the edge of the pot, it is an indication that potting on is necessary. Use a potting compost that contains lots of peat, leafmould and a little fresh sphagnum moss.

Should the leaves require cleaning, this must be done with a soft sponge and clear water, as they are very easily damaged. Oil-based cleaners will give the leaves a transparent appearance that will in time cause them to rot, so they should not be used.

Pellaea rotundifolia
Button fern. Easy

One of the easiest and most popular ferns is *Pellaea rotundifolia* (button fern), which produces a dense mass of small, very dark green leaves on slender stems. This fern tolerates quite low temperatures, but does enjoy a mist of water sprayed over its foliage.

Adiantum
Maidenhair fern. Moderately easy

When all is said and done, possibly the most attractive, and certainly one of the most useful of all the ferns, is the maidenhair or adiantum. Many of the very pale green-coloured varieties, such as *Adiantum fragrans*, are exceptionally fine with their black wiry stems contrasting sharply and beautifully with the delicate foliage.

Overleaf In this elegant drawing room a few distinctive plants have been used to good effect as an integral part of the interior design. In a spacious room where the shape of a large plant can really be appreciated this is usually more effective than a much greater number of small plants.
1 *Dracaena deremensis*
2 *Howeia forsteriana*
3 Codiaeum

Unusual ferns
Among the pteris ferns there are many with quite extraordinary colouring, ranging from silver to almost white. Stiff and upright stems carry the foliage in an elegant manner, making the pteris splendid plants for inclusion in the mixed collection. An even temperature around 16°C (60°F) will suit these plants best.

Propagation of ferns
Many of the smaller ferns that grow in clumps can be increased by teasing the plant apart and planting the segregated pieces as individual plants. Acquiring and sowing spores is by far the cheapest method of increasing the varieties and numbers of your plants; it is not as complicated as it may seem. When the spores have ripened on the reverse of the leaf, the leaf can be carefully removed, placed in a paper bag and allowed to dry. The spores will fall from the leaf and they can then be sown on damp peat in a temperature of around 27°C (80°F).

CHAPTER 6
Architectural plants

Such a grand-sounding heading for a chapter as architectural plants conjures up thoughts of towering office blocks and vast carpeted foyers.

In recent years there has been a tremendous upsurge in the use of plants in offices, virtually hundreds of containers being put to use throughout open-plan interiors. In most cases the plants are maintained by specialist plant contractors who call regularly to ensure that plants are fed, watered, cleaned and generally kept in good order. Presuming that the contractor knows his job, the important requirement as far as plants are concerned is that there should be adequate temperature every day of the week and that there should be sufficient light for plants to grow successfully.

Certainly the term 'architectural plant' does suggest one of fairly substantial proportions, and they are, in most cases, set off to better advantage in more spacious surroundings. This need not imply, however, that they have no place in the home, as most of these plants are, in fact, sold in a variety of pot sizes. Indeed, homes with larger rooms and entrance halls do accommodate many of these larger plants, though sometimes to the exclusion of a piece of furniture.

The available range of specimen indoor plants, be they architectural or otherwise, is limited to comparatively few species and varieties. No doubt many more plants could be listed as having architectural merit, but this seems quite pointless knowing that they are almost unobtainable commercially. Only very few of the commercial houseplant growers are prepared to tie up capital in a long-term investment in specimen indoor plants, many of which take several years to mature. Because of their slow rate of development these plants are almost invariably costly purchases.

On the question of cost, the individual specimen plant may be expensive, but in the proper setting it is much more impressive than a nondescript collection of smaller plants, and in the end need not be much more costly than a selection of small plants. Also, a larger plant will be much easier to care for than a collection of smaller ones, which dry out quite rapidly in warm conditions.

Selecting & positioning

When selecting and positioning such plants, be it in the office or private house their suitability must be carefully considered. In respect of height, there should be a minimum of 2 to 3 ft of head room so that the plant has an opportunity to develop. Where spotlights are used to highlight aspects of interior decor, or the plants themselves, care must be taken to ensure that the plant is at least 4 ft away from the light bulb or reflector. If there is a continual flow of people past the plant or plants, then they should be placed well away from their general route. This is to protect them from being damaged by passers-by brushing against them, and to deter inquisitive fingers from handling the leaves in an effort to decide whether they are real or plastic!

Although architects are very capable people where building design is concerned, many of them are lamentably ill-informed in respect of plants and their requirements. Elsewhere I have discussed the general requirements of indoor plants and their positioning and have no wish to repeat my remarks here, except on one point, namely, the question of plant height in relation to the size of the pot in which the plant will be growing. When visualising a bold plant of some 8 to 10 ft in height or with a wide spread, there is no point in providing a match-box-sized container in which to house the pot, as is so often the case. For larger plants the absolute minimum size of container is one with a diameter of 12 in and a depth of not less than 10 in.

*Philodendron
bipinnatifidum*

One further point on containers; I feel that they should be portable when housing larger plants. This will save a good deal of perspiration if it is decided to reposition the plant. Boxes, or containers, mounted on castors will simplify matters so that a rearrangement of the plants can become a matter of course. Also, it makes life much easier for whoever has to do the cleaning when boxes can be moved around.

Araceae

Aroid family

The *Araceae* and *Moraceae* are the families which provide the majority of plants that can be defined as architectural, mainly on account of their larger leaves and more stately appearance. The aroids, *Araceae*, as well as including many of our bolder plants, also give us some of the most beautiful and delicate-foliaged hot greenhouse plants. Perhaps the most important aroid for this chapter is the well-known *Monstera deliciosa borsigiana*, Swiss cheese plant, (see page 41), sometimes wrongly referred to as *Philodendron pertusum*. The latter is, in fact, a plant with smaller leaves and a more erect habit of growth. Of all the many beautiful green-leaved plants in

cultivation, Mother Nature surely excelled herself when devising the serrated, and eventually perforated, monstera leaf. Positioned where space is ample and temperature adequate the monstera will give lasting service with comparatively little attention.

Philodendron bipinnatifidium
Easy

Another aroid of spreading habit, with green fingerlike leaves is *Philodendron bipinnatifidum* (see page 44). Mention has been made elsewhere of the semi-retired gardener at our local railway station, and his devotion to, and ability with, plants. Perhaps the *P. bipinnatifidum* in the parcel office was his most spectacular plant, and much of the success was due to the aerial roots being allowed to drink up as much water as they required, instead of, as so often happens, being allowed to hang limply in a dry atmosphere. This was made possible by placing the plant pot in one end of a zinc trough and encouraging aerial roots, as they developed, to have a free run in the moist gravel in the bottom of the trough. This, by the way, is an excellent method of encouraging aroids to produce really bold leaves: stand them on the edge of a pool or water tank and give the aerial roots free run in the water. By so doing it will be found that the actual compost in the pot requires only the bare minimum of water.

Unusual philodendrons

Other philodendrons I mention only briefly on account of their scarcity. *Philodendron wendlandii* is a compact green plant with a shuttle-cock arrangement of the leaves that radiate from a low central crown; and Burgundy is an excellent and tolerant variety which will, in time, produce remarkably rich-coloured leaves, as much as 2 ft in length, in no way belying its name. This latter plant will benefit considerably if its supporting stake has a thick wad of sphagnum moss bound to it with florist's wire; keep the moss moist and aerial roots will quickly begin to work their way into the damp material. Similar in appearance to Burgundy but with plain green leaves, *P. hastatum* will also benefit from having its stake mossed; and, for the best results, the temperature should not be allowed to drop below 18°C (65°F).

Moraceae

Ornamental figs

The *Moraceae*, or fig family, provide us with an incredible range of ficus or rubber plants; from the creeping or climbing (if placed against a damp wall in the greenhouse) *Ficus pumila* to the majestic *F. lyrata* (see below). In the architectural group I have not included the upright *F. elastica decora*. Instead, one should endeavour to grow something rather more spectacular by acquiring one of these rubber plants when it has formed itself into a natural tree shape. This they do without help on reaching a height of about 8 ft, or when the growing tip has been deliberately cut out. Planted out into beds filled with good potting compost these plants will grow at a remarkable pace, putting on as many as 50 new leaves on a single branch in the course of one growing season.

Ficus lyrata

Fiddle-leaved fig. Moderately difficult
Ficus lyrata is an unusual and attractive plant, commonly named the fiddle-leaved fig because of its fiddle-shaped leaves. It will develop a sizeable trunk when at home in its surroundings. When well settled in and growing away it will tolerate quite severe pruning, though dark conditions and an inadequate or fluctuating temperature will quickly result in the loss of the lower leaves, and pruning will be more of a dream than a reality.

Ficus benjamina

Weeping fig. Moderately difficult
A ficus of quite different appearance, having nothing of the stiff habit of its relatives, is the elegant weeping fig, *F. benjamina*. This is often rather a perplexing plant when first put in position, as it seems almost inevitable that it will have some yellow leaves until it settles down. These should be removed, if only to improve the plant's appearance, and it will be found that in most cases the plant will establish itself in a week or two.

Besides the well known *Ficus benjamina* (weeping fig) we now have *F. benjamina nuda* that has more pointed leaves which hang much more gracefully. It is said to be more tolerant of indoor conditions, but in my experience it is little different. One of the problems with the weeping figs is that they take unkindly to being moved from one place to another, and have a tendency of showing their displeasure by shedding their leaves until they eventually settle down. The leaves of this plant may also turn brown and fall off if the growing location does not offer sufficient light. Although full sun is harmful, plants should nevertheless be placed reasonably near the light source, and certainly never in dark corners.

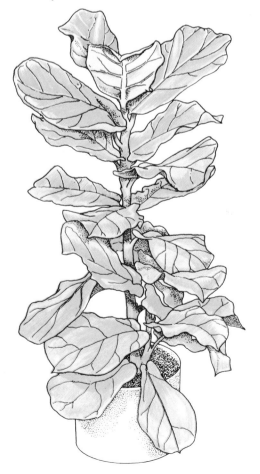

Ficus lyrata

Care of large ficus plants

Ficus plants in general should be inspected regularly when grown in pots standing on moist gravel or peat, as they are notorious for rooting through the holes in the bottom of the pot. This is one reason why it is often better to plant ficuses in boxes of compost where they can have a free root run, and grow much more rapidly and strongly as a result.

Being vigorous plants the majority of figs require regular feeding, and should be potted on once their roots have filled existing pots. A feeding programme similar to that recommended for the schefflera can also apply to the larger ficus plants. All of these will produce masses of roots that will make every effort to get out of the pot, either through the holes in the bottom or over the top, in the hope that there may be fresh soil for the plant to feed on. The weeping figs, once they have developed stems of reasonable circumference, will also have a tendency to produce thick roots from the stem of the plant. These are known as prop roots and act as very stout guy rope supports for plants when they are growing in their natural jungle environment.

Other suitable plants

A special favourite – Schefflera actinophylla

One of my particular favourites in the architectural range of houseplants, brings back fond memories of an old New Zealand friend, Mr Andrew Anderson. Many years ago he introduced the plant to me by writing the name *Brassaia actinophylla* on a greenhouse door and saying, with a finger stabbing at the name: 'This is a plant you must grow if you want specimen plants'. The plant, sold here as *Schefflera actinophylla*, deserves to be much more popular than it is, for it is a mixture of boldness and elegance; even a 15 ft specimen does not appear in any way heavy.

Negligence of either feeding or potting on when required will almost certainly have an adverse effect on schefflera plants, resulting in the loss of some lower leaves, and as there is no way of replacing these, the plant will forever look the worse for wear.

Feeding should be done regularly while the plant is in active growth. This could be continuously in a heated building and will mean feeding with a liquid feed about once each week. Alternatively, plants can be fed with plant food tablets that can be pressed into the soil. There they will gradually release beneficial nourishment to the roots. Usually purchased in a box of some kind, these tablets

Pandanus veitchii

come with full directions for their use – number of tablets required and frequency of application.

Not many pests attack the schefflera, but they are occasionally troubled by red spider mite, their presence being made known by a slight yellowing of the leaf. Treat with a proprietary insecticide.

Palms

Palms, like aspidistras, conjure up thoughts of the Victorian era and are not so popular today, though there are signs that they are returning to favour. Many of them make excellent indoor or office plants, and in a larger area well-grown plants of *Howeia belmoreana* or *Phoenix roebelenii* are well able to hold their own with more recent introductions. The lasting qualities of howeia are almost legendary; the phoenix is a little more difficult. Both require copious watering in the summer months, and regular potting on is essential, otherwise the mass of accumulated roots will begin to push the plant and compost upwards and almost out of the pot in time.

Pandanus

Screw pine. Easy

The vicious saw-edged leaf of the pandanus (the species *veitchii* is probably the best) make it essential that this plant should be positioned where passers-by will not come in contact with the leaves. Failure to do so frequently results in costly replacement of laddered tights! This is generally an easy plant to grow, and ideal for brightening up a plant display that is tending to become too green. To preserve the variegated colouring a light position is essential, and water should be given when the soil is seen to be dry and not as a daily ritual.

Dracaena
Easy and Difficult

For that exotic Palm Beach effect, few plants can compete with the dracaenas (unless it is a palm, of course), and in particular *Dracaena marginata*. It is a fairly easy 'doer', that in common with most dracaenas sheds its lower leaves as it increases in height. Far from being detrimental, this process often gives the plant a more elegant appearance, with its dull red-margined leaves spiking out in all directions.

Two more dracaenas that are somewhat more temperamental, so not for the novice, are *D. deremensis* and *D. massangeana*. The former, which has grey-green striped leaves, must have a minimum temperature of 18°C (65°F). Watering must also be done with great care; it must never be too wet or the leaves will brown at the tips and edges. *D. massan-*

geana, which will also test the grower's skill, has strap-like leaves, margined green with mustard-coloured centres. It is probably a more attractive plant when it has reached a height of 4 to 5 ft, and certainly it is better if given sufficient space for the leaves to spread naturally.

Tetrastigma voinierianum
Easy

Lastly, the tetrastigmas, and in particular the species *Tetrastigma voinierianum*, which excites the interest of those who prefer their plants to have interestingly shaped foliage. Certainly it has an advantage over most other large plants in that it is quick growing. In ideal greenhouse conditions 'rampant' is probably a better word as tetrastigmas are difficult to keep in check once they have decided to become entangled with their neighbours. As with ficuses, they too present difficulties when their roots decide to go in search of something other than that which is available in their pots. Growth is kept in check by frequently winding it back and forth around itself; string is unnecessary, as self-clinging tendrils quickly attach themselves to everything and anything. The compost should be kept moist and frequent feeding is essential. However, guard against excessive wet which results in leaves – and, in extreme cases, actual growing shoots – being shed.

Dracaena deremensis

CHAPTER 7
Flowering houseplants

Rather than write a few brief words about a huge number of plants, I have in this chapter on flowering houseplants, endeavoured to discuss some of the established favourites in more detail, and to include a selection of the plants that have become popular in recent years.

In general, the needs of flowering plants indoors are very similar to those of other plants, as described in the chapter on routine culture. The way in which some plants are inclined to shed flowers, and sometimes buds, when introduced to room conditions often gives rise for some concern. Much of the flower drop that occurs can be attributed to buffeting in transit, and to the change in conditions in respect of light and temperature. More often than not it will be found that plants quickly settle down in their new environment, and that flower production indoors presents few problems. However, permanently saturated compost and dark corners will result in weak growth and flowers that will drop at a touch.

There is no doubt that the condition of a flowering plant when purchased can influence its future life in the home. Unless flowers are especially wanted to create a favourable first impression, the plants should almost all be purchased at the earlier stage of growth – to be more specific, when they have some colour showing and an adequate supply of buds, formed and forming. There are a few exceptions, however, two of these being the pot chrysanthemum and the poinsettia. The latter should be well coloured and the chrysanthemum ought to have a good percentage of buds open, though not fully.

Achimenes
Hot water plant. Easy
The hot water plant, as it is commonly named, will start into growth in February much more readily if the rhizome is first soaked in hot water. Flowers in many shades are produced throughout the spring and summer months. Keep moist, cool and in good light and they will repay you with a continuous show of colour until plants naturally die down in late summer. Keep warm and dry over winter, and pot into fresh John Innes No. 2 or a soilless potting compost annually.

Anthurium
Moderately easy
Here we have further proof of the importance of the aroid family to the houseplant grower. The large-flowered (or, more accurately, large-spathed) *Anthurium andraeanum* requires a minimum temperature of 21°C (70°F), and a very humid atmosphere, so it is only suitable as a temporary room plant.

A very interesting variety, *A.* Guatamalan, is less demanding, needing a temperature of about 18°C (65°F) and less humidity. It is also more shapely, and the orange-red spathes are produced much more freely. (Though expensive, mature anthurium 'flowers' have a water life of five to seven weeks from the time of cutting).

Smaller and more compact than the previous types, *A. scherzerianum*, is, understandably, better known by its common name of flamingo flower. This plant does well in a light but not too sunny window, and appreciates a thoroughly well-drained and open compost. Soft water, with the chill taken off it, is preferred; and if at all possible, the room temperature should not drop below 16°C (60°F). Soil, as such, is not important, the main compost ingredients being peat, leafmould, fresh sphagnum moss and a little dried cow dung – the object being to prepare an open spongy mixture. Crock the pot, and add a few crocks to the potting mixture as well, to further assist drainage. To improve their appearance, the spathes should be supported by a thin cane or wire; if wire is used, make a loop at the top in which to rest the stem, placing the wire just below the coloured spathe.

Above left *Achimenes, the hot water plant*
Above right *Anthurium scherzerianum. Inset shows flower from A. andraeanum*

Aphelandra
Difficult

There is little to choose between *Aphelandra* Brockfeld and *A. squarrosa* Louisae. The former has more attractive foliage and the leaves are stiffer and carried almost horizontal to the main stem. The latter is less attractive in respect of foliage, but produces several yellow bracts to each stem, whereas Brockfeld is more inclined to have a single bract.

Both varieties are, without doubt, among the most trying of indoor flowering plants to care for. Dry roots and starvation are the main causes of failure, and these need be neglected on only one occasion for irreparable damage to be done. Aphelandras fill their pots with roots in a remarkably short space of time, so, from the moment they are purchased, they need lots of water and lots of fertiliser (the manufacturer's recommended dilution can be slightly exceeded for aphelandras and no harm will be done).

Azalea
Indian azalea. Easy

The pot-grown Indian azalea is one of our most attractive plants, and is available in many colours for about six months of the year, from November onwards. At no time must it be allowed to dry out, and frequent syringing of the foliage will help to create the moist atmosphere that is so important to its well being. It is one of the few plants that one can be quite specific about in respect of watering. When purchased, almost all of the larger plants are in effect miniature standard specimens,

having a short woody stem between pot and foliage. The properly watered plant should have a dark water mark about half way up this stem; if there is no mark the plant is too dry, and if the mark is near where the branches begin it is too wet. It is as simple as that.

Dead flowers should be removed regularly, and when the flowers have finished the plant is placed in a cooler room where it will require less water. During May, when frosts are less likely, the plant should be plunged to its pot

Azalea plants should be plunged in the ground outdoors when flowering has finished

rim in a sunny position in the garden, or in an airy cold frame that can have its cover removed during the day. Keep the compost moist and feed with liquid fertiliser during the summer months, when the foliage should also be sprayed over regularly. Before frosts are likely the plant must be moved into a cool room; and when buds begin to form, warmer conditions will encourage their development. When the plant is in flower the temperature can be reduced. The first year after purchase a plant might not flower so well, but once adjusted to the suggested routine it will provide a remarkable annual show of colour.

Begonia
Moderately easy
The humble green ivies are bought in huge numbers yet a serious attempt to popularise plants of the *Begonia corolicta*, *B. daedalea* and *B. mazae* types met with utter failure some years ago. Perhaps the public distrusted their fine foliage and exotic blooms. My experience suggests that these suspicions are quite unfounded, as I have successfully grown a selection of fibrous begonias over the years and find them less demanding than many of the houseplants normally considered.

At present the majority are in short supply, and so are difficult to acquire, but I feel that in time these plants will be given a second chance by the nurseryman, and they will then be more readily accepted by more knowledge-able and adventurous houseplant enthusiasts.

Some, such as *B. fuchsioides*, *B. lucerna* and *B. corolicta* become too large for the average room in time, but they almost all propagate with ridiculous ease, so there is no difficulty in starting a few fresh plants. All must have ample feeding when they are established, and potting on into larger containers should be made a spring chore.

Beloperone guttata
Shrimp plant. Easy
Much of the popularity of *Beloperone guttata* is due to the apt common name of shrimp plant, which it gets from the shrimp-like appearance of the dull orange-coloured bracts (the flowers are inconspicuous). Although normally quite small, reaching a height of about 18 in indoors, *Beloperone guttata* can be grown into a specimen plant in a comparatively short space of time. Some years ago, at the Paris Floralies, my eyes seemed to deceive me when I saw a shrimp plant of at least 5 ft in height, with a diameter of at least 3 ft and bracts almost 6 in in length. Later I had the good fortune to meet an employee of the

Beloperone with its shrimp-like flower bracts

nursery responsible for growing this monster. Taking his advice, an experiment was carried out, and we grew plants from a height of 12 in in 5-in pots in the May of one year to over 4 ft in 8-in pots by May of the following year. Regular feeding and potting on were the answer, plus the fact that all bracts were removed as they appeared, so preventing the plant using up energy in their production. (A useful tip for many flowering plants – build up a plant before allowing it to bloom). These plants were grown in a heated greenhouse, and would be an impossibility indoors, I imagine!

The feeding lesson can, however, still apply to the window-sill plant, but it is better to feed in spring and summer when new leaves are being produced. When bracts lose their attractiveness they should be removed, and at the same time plants can be pruned to a better shape. Firm trimmings, about 3 in in length, are not difficult to root if placed around the edge of small pots filled with John Innes No. 1 potting compost or a soilless cutting compost.

Chrysanthemum
Easy
By using artificial light to extend winter day length, or by covering the plants with black polythene in summer to shorten the day, the nurseryman is able to offer pot-grown chry-santhemums on any day of the year. Also, by incorporating growth-depressant chemicals in the potting mixture, the height of the plant can be restricted to between 15 and 20 in. Such plants should be purchased when showing a reasonable amount of colour and never when in tight bud. A good-quality plant in a 5-in pot will have about 20 flowers and can almost be guaranteed to last for a full six weeks indoors.

After flowering, they can be planted out in the garden, but, no longer being influenced by the chemical restriction on growth, the plant will attain the height of a normal garden chrysanthemum. Indeed, if planted out in time for the plants to develop a reasonable length of stem, it is possible for them to flower in their pots in the early part of the year, and for the same plants to flower later in the garden.

Cyclamen
Moderately easy

Almost all plants grown commercially are raised from seed and may take anything from 12 to 18 months before producing enough flowers to be considered saleable. During the major part of this time the plants are kept at a temperature in the region of 13°C (55°F) and ventilators are opened on every favourable occasion, so providing cool, airy conditions for most of the time. For seed germination the temperature is in the region of 21°C (70°F).

Having spent its entire life in light and airy surroundings, it is not surprising that a cyclamen plant quickly reacts against hot, dry room conditions by producing sickly yellow leaves and drooping flowers. A cool, light room provides ideal surroundings. Watering should be done thoroughly, allowing the compost to dry out (but never to become bone-dry) before watering again. The corm will not be damaged by water, but care must be taken not to get water in amongst the flower and leaf stalks, as they are inclined to rot.

A neighbour, who could keep a cyclamen in perfect health for anything up to five months, always swore by, and performed, a weekly ritual that she remembered reading of some years before. It involved having a bowl of about 12 in in diameter, in the centre of which she placed a block of wood about $1\frac{1}{2}$ in in thickness. Water was then poured into the bowl so that it did not quite cover the surface of the block when this was held down in the centre of the bowl. The cyclamen pot was then placed on the wood, which remained permanently moist. Each Saturday morning the moment of the week arrived when boiling water was poured from a kettle onto the block of wood – enough to replace the amount of water lost to the atmosphere during the week. When required, the compost in the pot was watered in the usual way. Though the purist may frown – and I cannot decide whether to approve or not – the cyclamen obviously liked this treatment.

For every success there must surely be a score of failures when attempting to keep cyclamen corms from one year to the next. It does seem, however, that once a corm has been successfully treated in this way it can be kept for a number of years without too much bother. Under normal conditions, the plant so treated is seldom as good as those grown from seed in the greenhouse. Nevertheless, there is a sense of satisfaction when success is achieved, so the following advice is offered. When the flowers have finished and the leaves begin to yellow and fall, water should be gradually reduced until the soil is quite dry. For preference the corm is left in its pot, which is placed on its side under the staging in the greenhouse. If a greenhouse is not available, a cool room or sheltered corner outside is the next best thing. In May, the plant should be knocked out of its pot and some of the old soil carefully removed and replaced with John Innes No. 2 potting compost. The plant can be left outside until mid-September when it is gradually introduced to warmer conditions (too sudden a change of temperature can be damaging). When the plants are established, they should be fed with liquid fertiliser.

Fuchsia
Moderately easy

Not the best indoor flowering plants as they have an essential need for maximum light, in

Fuchsia

the absence of which they will shed flowers and buds alarmingly. A full-light location is needed – plants will often be happier on the window ledge outside rather than in. Easily raised from cuttings, plants in a marvellous range of colours can be obtained, and they will flower endlessly throughout the late spring, summer and into early autumn if kept moist, well-fed, and in good light. A superb, trouble-free plant for the conservatory or small greenhouse.

Hibiscus
Easy
These are excellent room plants that will greatly benefit from being exposed to the maximum amount of sunshine, though the temperature need only be moderate. The exotic flowers last for a day or two only, but as one dies there always seems to be another in bud promising pleasure on another day. Correct watering is important; the compost must not at any time be allowed to dry out during the summer months, as loss of flowering buds will be the inevitable result.

My plant of *Hibiscus rosa-sinensis* is about 4 ft in height and is kept in check by annual pruning in the autumn when it is obvious that no further flowers can be expected until the following spring. The variegated form, *H. rosa-sinensis cooperi*, has red flowers that appear infrequently. The graceful habit and light colouring suggests, however, that it may well be a promising plant for the future. A cool, light place is most suitable, as plants will lose much of their bright colouring if temperatures are high and light is restricted.

Left *Hibiscus*

Right *Hoya carnosa variegata*

Hoya
Wax plant. Moderately easy
Much prized for its exquisite, pendant clusters of flowers, *Hoya carnosa* is, nevertheless, not

Hydrangea

an easy plant to flower indoors. It is best planted out in the greenhouse, or conservatory, with the growth trained to overhead wires. The flowers will then be better appreciated and will also be more plentiful.

Hoya carnosa variegata is even more reluctant to produce flowers when its roots are confined to a pot, but the attractive foliage more than compensates for lack of flowers. Some of these have better coloured foliage than others, and it may well be worth while looking through your supplier's stocks in order to locate those with a pink flush of colouring. In common with all climbing plants, hoyas will benefit if supports can be provided for growth to twine around.

Hydrangea
Easy
The hydrangeas are ideal dual-purpose plants, obtainable in shades of pink, red, white and blue, though the blue colours are in fact pink varieties that have been induced to change colour by adding carefully controlled quantities of alum to the potting soil. Never allow them to dry out, feed them well and they will be little trouble if given a light position. When flowering has finished indoors they can be planted outside hence the 'dual purpose'.

When planting out it is advisable to select a protected location so that young buds are not damaged by spring frosts. Plants being kept in their pots for growing on indoors or on the terrace should be pruned back in September, kept on the dry side and offered protection from frost over winter.

John Innes No. 3 compost should be used for potting, with a bluing agent such as alum being added to pink plants if one wishes to experiment with producing blue colours. Getting the ideal blue colouring is a highly skilled operation and will entail a degree of experiment before finding the correct amount of bluing agent to add to your particular soil.

The pure white *H. macrophylla* Soeur Thérèse has few peers and one of the best deep pinks is *H. macrophylla* Alpengluehn. A pink variety that 'blues' effectively is *H. m.* Bodense.

Hypocyrta
Clog plant. Easy
This is a comparatively new introduction and makes an interesting addition to the range of flowering houseplants. It is commonly named the clog plant on account of the attractive orange-coloured flowers that resemble a miniature clog. Even when not in flower the mass of glossy, dark green leaves are an attraction in themselves and, provided it receives the standard treatment for indoor plants, it is not difficult to care for. Growth may be trimmed into shape at almost any time after flowering and if used as 3-in-long cuttings, the healthy trimmings will root readily. One or two of the lower leaves should be removed before inserting. It is an excellent choice for growing in a container or basket suspended from the ceiling near a light window.

Temperature-wise one should aim for a minimum during the winter months of around 16°C (60°F), with summer temperatures not mattering so much, provided rooms do not become excessively hot and dry. In summer it is also important to ensure that the soil remains moist without becoming totally saturated, while in winter drier conditions are better. Feed regularly while in active growth but be careful not to overfeed.

Impatiens
Busy lizzie. Easy
Ease of propagation has established the busy lizzie (*Impatiens sultanii*) as one of our most popular and homely flowering plants. They root quite quickly, either in a proper compost or placed in water, and it is interesting to grow them in a clear glass bottle so that roots can be

Increasing humidity

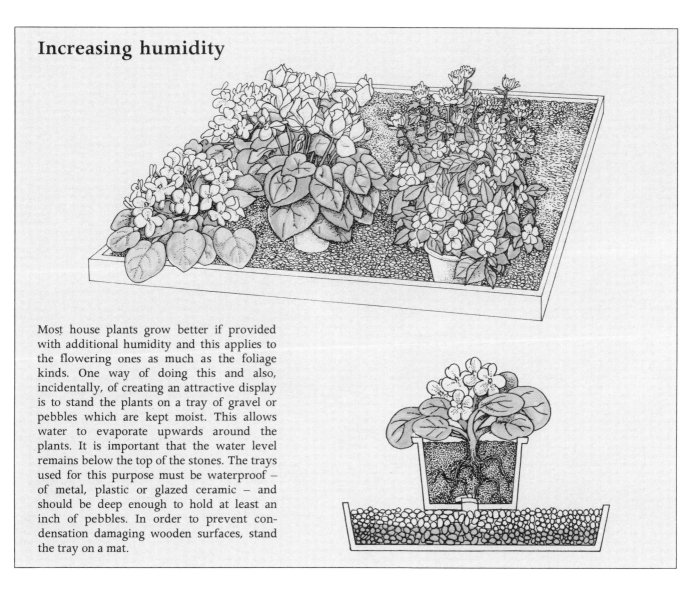

Most house plants grow better if provided with additional humidity and this applies to the flowering ones as much as the foliage kinds. One way of doing this and also, incidentally, of creating an attractive display is to stand the plants on a tray of gravel or pebbles which are kept moist. This allows water to evaporate upwards around the plants. It is important that the water level remains below the top of the stones. The trays used for this purpose must be waterproof – of metal, plastic or glazed ceramic – and should be deep enough to hold at least an inch of pebbles. In order to prevent condensation damaging wooden surfaces, stand the tray on a mat.

observed as they begin to grow. For growing plants a light sunny window is the place, and they should not be allowed to dry out, otherwise the flowers and buds will drop. They can be trimmed and reshaped at any time, and require regular feeding when in active growth if the leaves are to be kept healthy and green. If you want a plant as large as the one seen in the window down the road, pot your plant into a larger container using moist John Innes No. 2 potting compost or a soilless potting compost.

The newer species *Impatiens petersiana*, with dull red leaves and scarlet flowers will require more than the usual amount of fertiliser and more frequent potting on. A watchful eye should be kept on this impatiens for red spider; leaves becoming brown and dry are signs of their presence.

Besides raising new plants by means of cuttings, there is a wide range of F_1 varieties

that can be raised from seed with little difficulty. Resultant plants will be much more compact than the older varieties and the colour range of flowers much more extensive.

For something new and an alternative to seed, early in the year I purchase the rooted cuttings of the range of impatiens referred to as New Guinea Hybrids. The majority of these have names relating to the circus, Big Top, Trapeze and so on, and will develop into plants of quite amazing size and colour if they are potted on into John Innes No. 3 compost and fed regularly once the plants are established.

While in active growth impatiens must never be allowed to dry out and a careful watch should be kept for greenfly, which seems to find the soft, succulent busy lizzie especially appetising. If aphids are discovered spray with soapy water or, if the attack is more severe, with malathion or liquid derris.

Ipomoea
Morning glory. Easy
Raised from spring-sown seed the morning glory is a fine annual plant for training around a windowframe during the summer. Intense blue, trumpet-shaped flowers last for one morning as the common name suggests, but the flowering period spreads over several days. Easily managed if kept cool, light and moist.

Ipomoea, morning glory

Poinsettia
Christmas flower. Moderately easy
Poinsettias have green leaves and insignificant flowers that are surrounded by brightly-coloured bracts, which are actually coloured leaves. The red-coloured plant is best known, though there are equally good white, pink and cream-pink varieties available. The modern poinsettia is surely one of the most remarkable plants of recent years. It has now lost its too-delicate-for-words image and become an established favourite that is thoroughly reliable. A sweeping statement, maybe (I know there are still some that fail inexplicably), but the way in which the public and florist alike have accepted the variety Paul Mikkelsen is abundant proof of its durability.

Although the greenhouse cultivation of this variety is in itself a fascinating subject, I will only very briefly comment on this aspect. New techniques and the use of growth-depressant chemicals are responsible for the compact plant, seldom more than 24 in tall, that is today offered for sale. Intense red bracts are no longer confined to the pre-Christmas months of the year, as the nurseryman is able to use black polythene to restrict the amount of light available to the plant, so inducing it to flower at an unnatural time. As with chrysanthemums, poinsettia flower buds initiate (that is first begin to form) when the day reaches a given length, and when grown naturally the poinsettia does so in about the third week of October. The light factor is probably the most important single reason why it is difficult to flower poinsettias indoors. In the home, they usually have the normal day length of light and are then subjected to an additional five to six hours of artificial light in the evening. Plants therefore continue to grow instead of developing flowers and bracts. The answer is to grow them in a room where they only get natural daylight. A sunny window will be ideal and will only be too hot for them on the very brightest of days. A temperature of around 16°C (60°F) will be perfectly adequate.

A golden rule with watering is to water when necessary and not at set times, nor just for the sake of it. Feeding is not important once the bracts have formed; before this, apply weak liquid fertiliser regularly.

Reports indicate that it is possible to have plants in colour for eight months or more from the time of purchase. This would, however, be the exception, and one would normally expect a flowering time of between six and eight weeks.

As the flowers in the centre of the bract begin to rot, or drop off, the bract itself will gradually begin to disintegrate. At about this time, the leaves will also begin to turn yellow and will fall at a touch. When the plant is no longer attractive the main stem should be cut back to a height of about 6 in from the soil surface. The flow of sap from the cut stem will do no harm and can either be left to dry naturally or can be checked by applying powdered charcoal or moist sand to the wound.

A week or two before cutting the stem, water should be gradually reduced until the compost is almost dry. If not considered unsightly, the plant can remain in the window; failing this it should be stored in a warm place, as cold conditions will lessen its chance of survival. While it is resting, the compost must be kept almost dry until new growth appears, when normal watering can be gradually resumed. At this time the plant can be potted on, or re-potted in the same pot after first removing some of the old soil; John Innes No. 2 potting compost is the best to use. If the plant is successfully flowered for a second time one should not expect indoor growth to produce quite such large bracts as those of greenhouse-grown plants.

Saintpaulia

African violet. Moderately easy

In the fascinating world of horticulture there is no plant that has caught the imagination and interest of the houseplant grower more than the humble African violet. It is without a doubt one of the most widely cultivated potted flowering plants. One good reason for their popularity is that they can flower throughout the year.

Since the first *Saintpaulia ionantha* was removed from its mountainside in Tanzania there has been a quite phenomenal amount of hybridising done. There must now be several thousand varieties of saintpaulia listed as distinct varieties, but it would be very foolish even to suggest that all of them are available, only the best are retained.

Besides variations in flower colour and shape, there is also a considerable difference between the varieties in the colour, shape and general appearance of many of the leaves: a comparatively recent and very pleasing introduction from Denmark has been *S. rococo* in both blue and pink colours. The flowers are an attractive semi-double and the leaves are particularly interesting for their shorter stalks

and the contrasting pale green colouring where the leaf is attached to the petiole. These would seem to constitute an interesting new strain which will encourage further developments and improvements in the same way as other positive strains have done such as the varieties developed from the Holtkamy Rhapsody strain from Germany and the Balli strain from America. Most of the plants within these groups have, like racehorses, retained the essential characteristics of the parents. So, rather than present a lengthy list of difficult-to-obtain plants, I would suggest that one should contact a good supplier to see what is available. Alternatively, join a group that has African violets as a special interest, and you may well be able to participate in a plant exchange arrangement.

African violets are among the most perplexing of all our indoor plants, and almost everyone seems to have attempted growing them at one time or other. Most people shake their heads in disbelief when they see a really well-flowered plant, saying they have tried saintpaulias unsuccessfully so many times. The natural follow-up question is, 'What is the secret?'

Mrs Murray, an old friend and true expert on the subject, attributes her success to a mysterious ingredient which she refers to as TLC – tender, loving care. Though TLC is important, there is a great deal more to it than that, as our expert well knows. To achieve success there are, to my mind, three essential factors that cannot be ignored: light, adequate temperature and proper watering.

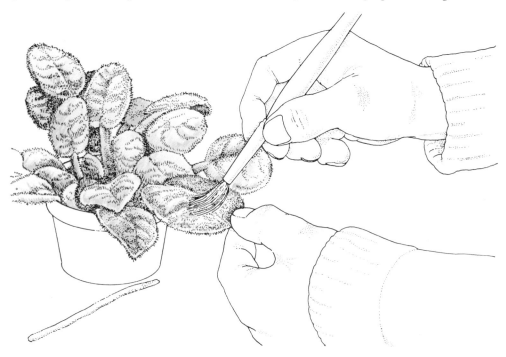

African violet leaves should be gently cleaned with a soft brush

According to most of the recognised experts, saintpaulias should have approximately 14 hours of light each day. So it is a question of the lightest possible window during the day, and supplementary artificial light in the evening. I have found that most of the greatly improved strains of saintpaulia now on sale will do perfectly well on a sunny window-ledge, needing protection from only the strongest mid-day sun. Have a care, though; sunshine on wet leaves will be damaging, so avoid wetting leaves when watering.

Often I have listened to the tale of woe as someone has described how wonderfully well their African violet did in the steamy kitchen window during the summer, only to gradually succumb with the approach of winter. It is the common fault of inadequate temperature that is responsible for leaves becoming darker in colour and beginning to shrivel as cold conditions and fluctuating temperatures have their effect. Although plants will survive at lower temperatures, I have found that a minimum of 18°C (65°F) is essential if plants are to be in good health and produce fresh leaves at the same time.

Some time ago, on recommending the use of tepid water for saintpaulias, I was just a trifle nonplussed when a listener, in all seriousness, asked where it could be purchased! As hot water can be more harmful than cold, care should be taken to use water that has just got the chill off; I find that a container of water placed in a warm room overnight is ideal for use the following morning. Water must be kept off the leaves and away from the central crown of the plant, and is best given by placing the pot in a shallow saucer of water and allowing the plant to drink up all it requires before tipping away the surplus. Never allow plant pots to stand in water for any length of time.

Damaged leaves and dead flowers must be removed as soon as they are seen in order to prevent rot setting up in the centre of the plant. When cleaning plants in this way, it is important that the complete leaf or flower stalk should be removed, leaving no pieces that are likely to rot if left attached to the plant.

Cuttings present little difficulty: firm, clean leaves are inserted in a peat and sand mixture. Endeavour to maintain a temperature in the region of 18°C (65°F). They will also form roots in water. When the young plants clustered around the parent leaf are large enough to handle, and have a reasonable amount of root attached, they should be gently teased apart. A number of individual little plantlets will result; handled carefully, these can be potted up individually, or spaced out in a seed box filled with a mixture of two-thirds John Innes No. 2 potting compost to one-third clean peat or a soilless potting compost. (This mixture will be suitable for saintpaulias at all stages of growth). Treated in this way, plants with single crowns will result and flowers will stand boldly away from the overlapping rosette of neat leaves. If left undivided flowers and leaves intermingle and present a less attractive plant. In order to build up strong plants it is advisable to remove the first, and sometimes the second, flush of flowers; by so doing the plant's energy will be directed to leaf development, and it will, in turn, flower more freely.

Spathiphyllum wallisii
White sails. Moderately easy
Protection from direct sunlight is essential if one is to succeed with this aroid, and the compost must never be allowed to dry out if the glossy green leaves are to retain their appearance. Regular feeding and annual potting on in early spring are two more essentials that will have to be attended to if plants are to remain in good fettle. Propagation, by division of the root clumps, is not difficult, and may be done at almost any time other than when plants are in flower. The stiffly erect, creamy-white flowers are ever popular with

Spathiphyllum wallisii

the florist and flower arranger; even when they have dulled to green they still have an attraction for some.

Strelitzia

Bird of paradise flower. Easy
Strelitzia reginae is a plant bearing a splendid proper name and an equally fascinating common name – bird of paradise – derived from the bird-like appearance of the exotic blue and orange flower. The combination of name and flower, brings the plant immediately to notice but it really is not the best of plants to have indoors. The leaves are unattractive, and in order to produce its long-awaited flower, plants must be in very large pots.

Seed is generally freely available and is not difficult to germinate, but from seed it will probably take at least six years (or more) for plants to produce flowers. They require a fairly heavy potting mixture, such as John Innes No. 3, cool, light conditions indoors, and a full sun location out of doors in the summer. Water freely, giving a little less in winter. Pot on when roots push out of the pot.

Streptocarpus

Cape primrose. Easy
This plant is a particular favourite of mine. The variety Constant Nymph freely produces violet-blue flowers throughout the spring and summer and never fails to attract attention. Besides the blue, there is also a white form of *S.* Constant Nymph which offers a pleasing contrast. Possibly the most important step in respect of hybridisation of these plants has been taken by the John Innes Institute who have produced many more compact varieties in a splendid range of colours. They all have girls names: 'Tina' with magenta markings; 'Fiona' which is pink with a white throat and 'Diana' which also has a white throat and is principally cerise in colour. Perhaps the greatest difficulty will be in locating a source of supply, as the brittle leaves that overlap in the pot make it almost impossible to pack without damage and nurserymen are loth to grow it. Probably the best answer is to try your local nursery, which does not have to contend with packing problems. Failing this, find an owner who is willing to sacrifice a medium-sized, healthy leaf from his plant. The lower portion of the complete leaf, inserted in propagating compost, will be reasonably easy to root. Alternatively, new plants will not be difficult to raise by division, splitting older clumps after they have flowered and potting them in John Innes No. 2 compost or a soilless potting compost, or by growing them from seed sown in heat in January.

Orchids

Streptocarpus

Many orchid plants are much tougher than is often supposed, and considering that many of them are epiphytes, it goes without saying that they must have a tough constitution to survive in the extremes of wet and dry conditions that must prevail in their natural habitat.

There are orchids that like cool conditions, those that like to be on the warm side and countless others that fall between. It is therefore impossible to recommend ideal temperatures. This very diverse and extensive family of plants makes generalisation very difficult, but for the easier plants that one may care to try indoors it can be said that a temperature in the region of 16°C (60°F) should be the aim. Also, a light, airy and humid location should be provided, and any potting should be done with a properly prepared orchid mixture that drains very freely and offers maximum aeration.

The best indoor orchids that I have seen were growing in a deep window that had been built out from the house, so that it resembled a small greenhouse attached to the wall – a sort of bay window at conventional windowledge height. In such a window the plants can be provided with their own micro-climate, the glass can be shaded to offer protection from the sun and a great deal can be done to incorporate the maximum number of plants by suspending them from the roof and around the walls. Likewise, there are numerous plant cases of reasonable size available in which

continued on page 108

Flowering pot plants provide a long-lasting source of pleasure especially in winter when cut flowers are scarce
Far left A large azalea plant in full bloom is a blaze of colour
Left Chrysanthemums are always popular gifts and can be planted out in the garden after flowering indoors
Below The humble impatiens (busy lizzie) will grow into an impressive plant with good care and the regular pinching out of the shoot tips

plants can be provided with specialised conditions that are quite different to those prevailing in the room in which they are located. In more temperate regions plants can be placed out of doors in a warm and sheltered area during the summer months.

The indoor orchid requires a fairly high humidity level in the region of 70 per cent, which will mean frequent misting of the foliage with a fine spray of tepid water. With individual pots on window sills it is difficult to maintain humidity, so it becomes necessary to provide a tray of some kind filled with moistened gravel on which plants can stand.

In better equipped commercial establishments, new plants are propagated from seed and are raised in highly specialised conditions that would be far beyond the means of anyone other than the specialist grower. For example, from the time of germination, seedlings of cattleyas will take five to seven years before they eventually produce flowers – one of the reasons for the plants being costly. A simpler method used with many varieties that will result in much earlier flowering is to remove mature pseudobulbs and plant them up individually, or by dividing actual clumps of plants and potting them individually. Cattleyas, cymbidiums and paphiopedilums (the comparatively easy slipper orchid) are examples of plants that can be increased by division.

Angraecum sesquipedale

A plant well worth considering if the owner is prepared to sell you one, certainly a nice name to roll off the tongue. I include it here out of sheer devilment. I have been reading that it is a plant for the stove greenhouse (temperature around 21°C (70°F)), yet I recall growing this plant in a sort of slatted wooden box in very spartan conditions and it did splendidly. The foliage is very ordinary, but the glistening white flower with an extremely long white spur was a rare but regularly appearing sight in spite of the rough conditions. When in flower, it came indoors and was treated no differently than the many other indoor plants which surrounded it.

This plant, and its treatment and conditions of growing, is mentioned by way of encouragement to anyone who may be offered an orchid and is unsure of taking on something with the reputation for being exotic. Exotic maybe, but you could well be surprised by the manner in which many of these plants will settle down and do perfectly well indoors – perhaps giving the feeling that you have at last got a brush of the old greenfingers magic!

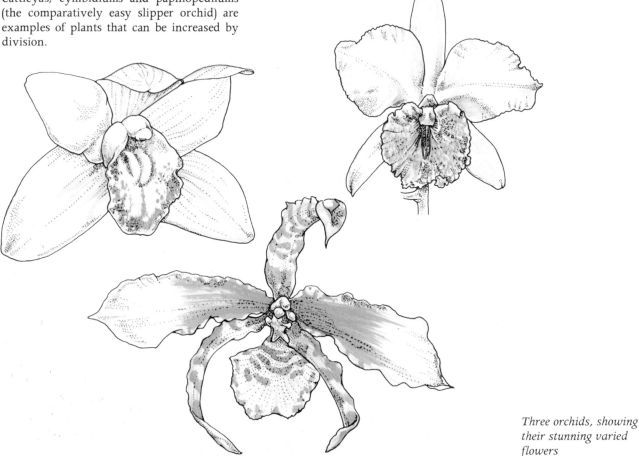

Three orchids, showing their stunning varied flowers

Cattleya

Anyone sufficiently interested could well set up a collection composed entirely of these very fine plants and the many hybrid forms, which are generally not difficult to obtain from the specialist grower. Plants rest in winter when less water is required, but the mixture in which they are growing must at no time become excessively dry. Provide a light growing position in winter and a spot that offers protection from strong sunlight in summer.

Cymbidium

These are the backbone of the orchid business, producing spectacular flower spikes in an infinite range of colours, particularly through the winter months. In time the plants become very large and require ample space, but they are not in the least difficult to care for as far as orchids go, and will tolerate a wide temperature range as long as there is a buoyant and airy atmosphere.

Compost must be free draining, and it is important to water thoroughly – for smaller pots that can be handled easily this will mean plunging the plant pot in a bucket of water and allowing all air bubbles to escape before the pot is removed. If flowers are to be cut they must first be allowed to open fully on the plant; individual flowers are much used in floristry.

Dendrobium

Very wide ranging with more than 1,000 species, many of which leave much to be desired when not in flower; the flowers do make up for any deficit there may be in the foliage. Higher temperatures are generally required, but there is some variation depending on the type, so it is well to get growing instructions with the plant when purchased.

Miltonia

For limited space and maximum pleasure this could well be the choice, not only as an orchid but as an indoor plant in general, certainly so if one possesses a heated conservatory. Those with flowers resembling pansies are especially attractive and could well be the perfect plants for that extended window 'greenhouse' mentioned earlier. Being epiphytic they can be used in many interesting ways other than as simple potted plants.

Odontoglossum

Allied to the miltonia and requiring a growing temperature in winter of about 16°C (60°F) minimum. Will do best in a lightly shaded moist atmosphere and can be propagated by division.

Overleaf Poinsettias have become the traditional 'Christmas flower' and so make excellent gifts. In recent years new varieties have been developed which are easier to look after than their predecessors and a whole range of colours is now available from white through all shades of pink to red. This photograph shows two extremes of the range – a greenish white and lovely rich red. When giving plants as gifts do not wrap them up too long in advance. Keep them in optimum conditions for as long as possible.

Paphiopedilum
Slipper orchid

A tongue twisting name for the slipper orchid which does well if kept moist in a lightly shaded, reasonably warm location. A small collection of different varieties provides a succession of flowers.

The attractive, pansy-like flower of miltonia

CHAPTER 8
Climbing and trailing plants

With houseplants, the aim is to have a variety of healthy plants displayed to their fullest possible advantage, and in this respect there cannot be anything better than an attractive trailing plant cascading from a hanging pot or basket.

Hanging baskets

An extensive selection of decorative pots has been developed to display on shelves, from wall brackets or be suspended from the ceiling. A natural extension of the latter has been the need to provide something to hold the pot in its mid-air position; macramé is the most popular solution. Macramé is the time absorbing craft of intricately weaving string and similar materials into all sorts of beautiful patterns (beautiful patterns may be a rather sweeping statement, as some of the creations done in heavier or synthetic materials can be quite hideous). However, the majority of the macramé items will enhance the appearance of the plant, the container and the room in which they are placed.

Multihangers, holding three or more pots are suitable for rooms with high ceilings, and must have firm anchorage; three pots with plants, soil and weight of water are surprisingly heavy and must have a stout hook from which to hang. The same applies to hanging baskets which will hold a number of plants.

Most decorative pots for hanging plants are without drainage, so care must be exercised when watering to ensure that the compost does not become too soggy. There are pulleys available with which one can raise and lower plants from their elevated positions. This feature is especially useful for heavier plants and will greatly simplify the business of watering – for one thing it will be much less hit and miss.

With hanging plants, both out of doors and in, it is better to have the container suspended at about head level, which will make it possible to regularly check the condition of the soil, without needing to find a stepladder first. When feeding hanging plants it is much easier to use fertiliser in tablet form – tablets are simply pushed into the soil at intervals as recommended by the manufacturer.

Watering hanging plants

Returning to watering, there are several ingenious devices available to assist with watering plants at higher levels. One in particular is useful for the person with a number of plants – a lightweight hosepipe is attached to the domestic water tap and at the other end there is an extension pipe for reaching the basket. Water is then controlled by the operator with a special on-off switch that works admirably. As with almost all houseplants, one should water hanging plants thoroughly and allow the soil to become reasonably dry before watering again.

Suitable plants for hanging baskets

Many ordinary houseplants will develop into fine climbers or trailing plants if their supporting stakes are removed so that they can trail downwards. Two of the best plants in this respect are the grape ivy, *Rhoicissus rhomboidea*, and the sweetheart plant, *Philo-dendron scandens* – both green foliaged plants that are better out of constant direct sunlight. In macramé hanging pots, a pleasing effect can be achieved with both these plants by allowing some of the strands to climb the string support, while the main part of the plant is allowed to trail naturally over the basket edge.

One of the very best trailing foliage plants for a position out of the sun is *Scindapsus aureus*; it is particularly suitable as a hanging plant when grown by one of the water culture methods. Growing plants by one of these

continued on page 116

Left A tower pot is a suitable container for a collection of saintpaulias (African violets) with their varying flowers and leaves. The cyclamen adds a splash of pink in the background
Top left The colourful bract and interesting leaves of anthurium
Top right A cymbidium orchid
Bottom right It is easy to see how *Strelitzia reginae* acquired the common name 'bird of paradise flower'

methods in an elevated position is something that has not been taken full advantage of. Control of watering is very simple, and the water indicator in the container can be so located that one should be able to read it from floor level.

If offered a light position in the window, many of the busy lizzies (impatiens) do splendidly in hanging containers. Not requiring quite so much light, but needing even temperature in the region of 18°C (65°F), *Columnea banksii* is a fine plant with oval shaped evergreen leaves, and a wealth of exotic orange flowers in early spring. These plants will usually flower more freely if the soil is kept on the dry side during January and February; at other times regular feeding and watering will be necessary.

The humble tradescantia in its several forms is the perfect trailing plant for the home; when they become a bit ragged around the top of the pot, as they invariably do, one can rectify the situation by inserting cuttings in the top of the pot to sprout afresh. Ivies for lighter and cooler rooms will also do well, and for warmer and slightly darker locations the creeping fig (*Ficus pumila*) is excellent, but it must at no time be allowed to become too dry.

Flowering trailers

Pendulous begonias, trailing varieties of fuchsia and *Campanula isophylla*, with its lovely star flowers, will only retain their flowers if offered good light. The first mentioned pair really being only suitable for the glassed-in porch or conservatory.

Climbers

To complement the hanging plants there are also a number of natural climbers that can be used for covering wall areas, or providing divisions of greenery between one part of a room and another. Most majestic and far and away the most popular of the climbing or upright plants is the monstera which tolerates a variety of conditions and treatment. Possibly tougher in its constitution and if anything more adaptable is *Rhoicissus rhomboidea* which, as mentioned earlier, is quite prepared either to climb or trail down. For various methods of training see page 120.

Most rampant of the climbers is the vine *Tetrastigma voinierianum* which, if happy with its treatment, will almost seem to have continually moving growth as it covers the wall or supporting framework.

Cacti & succulents

Trailing cacti or succulents are also a possibility, with hearts entangled, *Ceropegia woodii*, providing a yard-long cascade of heart-shaped leaves that are primarily grey-green in colour. Though not having such long trails, the rat's tail cactus, *Aporocactus flagelliformis*, is interesting. *Sedum morganianum*, though not for the beginner, is an interesting trailing succulent with ropes of blue-grey leaves that are roughly tubular in shape.

Tetrastigma voinierianum

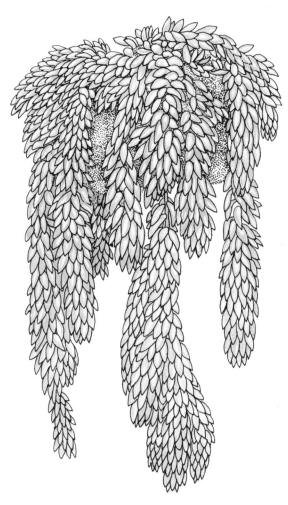

Ficus radicans
Difficult
To succeed with the variegated *radicans*, a propagating case or a damp mossed stake would appear to be essential, as plants quickly deteriorate in the dry atmosphere of the average room.

Suggested plants

Columnea
Moderately difficult
These and allied plants, such as aeschynanthuses (syn. trichosporums) are not too difficult despite their exotic flowers. Being naturally trailing in habit, they should be placed where growth will trail down and show the flowering bracts to better advantage when they appear. When older plants become untidy new ones may be started from cuttings rooted in moist peat in warm conditions; whole strands will root if laid on the surface of the peat.

Ficus pumila
Creeping fig. Easy
It is not always realised that the creeping fig, *F. pumila*, a charming green plant of easy culture, can be encouraged to climb if a mossed stake, or piece of cork bark, is provided for the aerial roots to cling to. It is essential that the support should be kept moist and equally important that the compost should not become saturated, so fill a scent spray with water and use this for damping the support.

Above left *Sedum morganianum*

Above right *Ficus radicans*

Trailing peperomias
Three trailing peperomias, ideal for edging plant troughs and containers, are *P. scandens*, *P. glabella variegata* and the more recently introduced *P. tithymaloides*, which has mottled green and gold variegations. The latter produces occasional green shoots that are not unattractive and, indeed, help to set off the variegation. No more than three or four green pieces need be left, as any more would quickly outgrow the more colourful pieces.

Platycerium alcicorne
Stag's horn fern. Moderately easy
One of my favourite houseplants, the stag's horn fern, as it is called, is much less difficult indoors than its appearance at first sight suggests.

As the platyceriums are epiphytes, better results will be achieved if plants are attached to a piece of bark, or absorbent timber; or they can be planted in an old log or tree stump. The method employed is the same as that described for cryptanthus (see page 53). Once established on their anchorage, platyceriums can remain there literally until they grow

continued on page 121

Climbing and trailing plants
offer a great deal of scope
for decorative ideas
Left *Philodendron scandens*
is a very versatile plant and
has been used here in a
fun, jungle-type
arrangement, giving an idea
of what it would look like in
its natural environment
Right As a contrast a trailing
plant, columnea, is used to
good effect in a light
conservatory

Training plants

Imaginative training of climbing plants greatly increases their scope for use as display features in room decoration. The following are some of the most popular methods: 1. The simplest way is to twine the stems round a single cane. 2. A plant can be trained up a small trellis which can be bought ready-made or constructed from canes firmly tied together. 3. A larger trellis can be used to create a leafy room divider or wall decoration. 4. The stem of the plant can be wound round two canes in S-shaped loops. 5. Some plants can be trained successfully round a circular loop of strong plastic-coated wire.

When training plants in this manner handle them carefully; remember that if a stem is broken or bent at too acute an angle the flow of sap will stop and the plant die off above the break. Tie stems to the support with twine or paper- or plastic-covered plant ties, choosing whichever blends best with the plant's natural colour.

For best results choose a fast-growing plant such as *Cissus antarctica, Rhoicissus rhomboidea* or *Tetrastigma voinierianum.* Stephanotis is a suitable plant to grow round a circular hoop.

Platycerium alcicorne

it is most essential that a moist support be used into which the plant can work its roots.

Stephanotis floribunda
Madagascar jasmine. Easy

The heavily scented flowers of this plant are an almost indispensable part of the better-quality bridal bouquet. The scent of only a few 'pips' indoors will find its way into every room – unless, of course, you happen to live in a mansion. I am experimenting with a plant indoors at the moment, to see how it reacts to room conditions, but I have not had it long enough to form a proper opinion. Reports of great success from various owners of stephanotis plants have, however, surprised me; and there does not appear to be any special treatment, other than a light window position and a temperature of about 16°C (60°F). When training plant growth to supports use a trellis, or hooped wire, so that growth can be wound backwards and forwards, thus checking the flow of sap and encouraging flower development.

themselves out of house room. As some indication of their potential, I once measured a plant that was 6 ft in length and the same across. The hanging basket in which it had been originally planted had long since disappeared in the heart of the plant.

When attached to bark it is usual for stag's horn fern to be hung on the wall so that their antler appearance can be set off to full advantage. There is an obvious precaution, however; the wall must be made of brick, or some other material that will not be harmed by moisture.

Watering is simply done by plunging both plant and anchorage in a bucket of water and allowing the surplus water to drain away before putting it back in position. A little liquid fertiliser mixed into the water is beneficial, care being taken that the fertiliser is used according to the manufacturer's instructions.

Scindapsus aureus
Money plant or devil's ivy. Moderately difficult

Scindapsus aureus is an attractive plant that will respond to the treatment generally recommended for philodendrons. With leaves of similar shape and shorter internodes than its parent, the variety Marble Queen lives up to its name for it has white marbled foliage. It is not an easy plant, the leaves being prone to browning at the edges when the plants are young and the roots weak. Once the plants have established themselves they are not so troublesome. When grown as an upright plant

Scindapsus aureus

The
Hall

Plants for the hall must be choosen with great care to suit the conditions in your own home. Remember that all plants hate a draughty position. The arrangement **below** would only suit a warm, draught-free hall. It includes *Ficus benjamina, Aechmea fasciata, Dracaena deremensis, Begonia rex* and *Nephrolepis exaltata*. A cool, light hall **(right)** makes a good home for a large fern, with a small leaved ivy and *Rhoicissus ellendanica* on the low window sill.

CHAPTER 9
Cacti and succulents

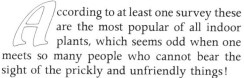ccording to at least one survey these are the most popular of all indoor plants, which seems odd when one meets so many people who cannot bear the sight of the prickly and unfriendly things!

Perhaps this popularity can be attributed to the ease of their propagation and, if one discounts the rare kinds, the fact that they are just about the easiest of all potted plants to care for. My own collection seems to thrive on minimal care. But the one sure way of killing them off is to provide conditions that are a combination of cold and wet. The majority of them, however, will not object too much to cooler temperatures provided they are not wet at their roots.

With such a wide-ranging family of plants it is difficult to generalise in respect of care and attention, but by the same token it would be impossible to cater for all their needs in these few pages. But, to be bold, may I suggest that indoors they should all have a light position in which to grow (most in full sunlight), and water that is given freely and regularly, say once weekly during the growing season. The growing season is usually from spring to autumn, during which period the compost should be kept moist. From about mid-October to early March the majority of them will be better without water. Temperature is not important provided it does not become excessively cold; average room conditions are fine.

This may seem spartan treatment, but it will keep plants in better condition, and a much greater number of plants in your collection will produce flowers during the following early spring and summer. The flowers of cacti and succulents can be a considerable bonus, as most have flowers of the most brilliant colouring, although some of them may last for a fleeting few hours only.

Because of the somewhat general advice in respect of plants and watering, it may be found that some plants which appear to be suffering as a result of the drought conditions will require a little water in winter, but it must never be excessive. Succulent types may need more water.

Given proper conditions and ripe seed many of these plants will germinate like mustard and cress and, if time is on your side, it is far and away the best and cheapest way of starting a collection. Compost for growing cacti is now freely available, and with the addition of a little extra sand this will be fine for seed sowing. A shallow seed box is the best container – the soil should be gently pressed into position and the seed sown thinly on the surface with perhaps a fine scattering of sand over the seed. Water it all with a very fine rose on the can, place a sheet of glass over the box, and then newspaper over the glass, and wait for the tiny seeds to sprout. Given reasonable warmth (in the region of 18°C (65°F) it will not be long before the box begins to fill with minute pinheads of growth that will in time develop into the weird and wonderful shapes we know so well. From a few packets of seed an amazing assortment will often result.

There is no urgency for removing the seedlings from the box – they can be left until they produce firm young plants that can then be potted into individual small pots using an appropriate porous cactus compost.

Propagated in this way, there will obviously be many duplicated varieties, and one then has to be selective in retaining only the best, perhaps donating the others to friends.

Fortunately, these plants are not much troubled by pests (other than overwatering on the part of the too attentive owner), though mealy bug, which manifests itself as a tiny ball of what appears to be cotton wool in the more

continued on page 128

Right A dish garden planted up with various kinds of succulents makes a long-lasting decoration

Opposite page
Top Cactus flowers come in a range of bright colours appropriate to their natural sunny surroundings
Bottom left The flower of *Schlumbergera gaertneri,* the Easter cactus
Bottom right An epiphyllum flower – Dobson's Yellow

inaccessible parts of the plant, can be a problem. The actual bugs have the appearance of tiny white woodlice – the young bugs being protected in the cotton wool-like substance. Dabbing methylated spirits onto the pests by means of a small paintbrush or piece of cotton wool tied to a matchstick will destroy them.

On a south-facing windowsill I have a 4-ft-long plastic window tray in which there is a layer of about three quarters of an inch of sand, and placed on the sand there are twenty square plastic pots holding one cactus each. These fill the tray perfectly making it a fine display. There are mammalarias, echinocactus, rebutia and similar plants of exquisite symmetrical shape, that give me immense pleasure. The south facing aspect is very hot and sunny in summer and often quite cool in winter, but these plants have proved to be the ideal occupants for the location.

On account of their prickly, inhospitable appendages some of the cacti are problem plants when it comes to potting them into larger containers, not that this is a frequent necessity. New pots should be only slightly larger than the old pots, and potting should be done in the spring. However, there may be the additional need to take the precaution of using a folded newspaper in the form of a collar to hold the plant while it is being placed in position. A properly prepared quick-draining compost is most essential.

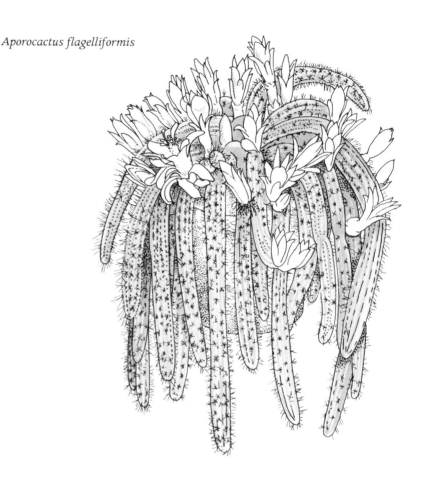

Aporocactus flagelliformis

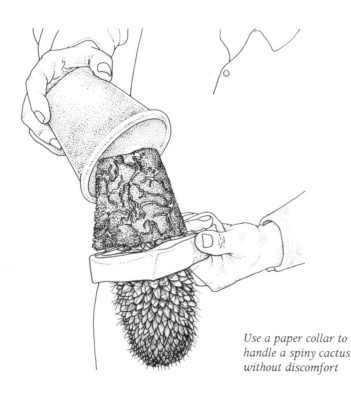

Use a paper collar to handle a spiny cactus without discomfort

Favourite varieties

The following list only scratches the surface, but could prove to be an interesting basis to a collection. Few are difficult, and most of them will add interest by producing flowers.

Aloe variegata
Partridge breast aloe
Commonly named partridge breast aloe on account of interesting variegation in shades of green. Flowers, borne on tall stems, are tubular and reddish orange in colour. Can be increased from seed or offsets, and requires no special care other than warmth and light.

Aporocactus flagelliformis
Rat's tail cactus
The rat's tail cactus may be grown in a hanging pot, as it has cylindrical trailing stems from which appear attractive hose-in-hose pink flowers of deep pink colouring. Requires reasonable winter warmth.

Cephalocereus senilis
Old man cactus
Slow growing and covered in long silvery hairs that give it the common name of old man

cactus. Would you believe that the hairs can be washed and combed when dirty? My own twenty-year-old plant has never had this treatment, but it is a fine specimen nevertheless, and no trouble to care for. Occasional watering, a light windowsill and an average temperature are all that it requires.

Cereus peruvianus

Easily-cared-for plant that will give some height to a collection. Develops into stereotype 'wide-open-spaces' cactus in time, with attractively ribbed stem. Besides this one there are any number of attractive cereus to choose from.

Crassula lycopodioides

Tiny leaves form branches of square and interesting stems that sprout further stems to eventually give a miniature tree-like effect. Flowers are insignificant, but it is a trouble free plant that is easily propagated from pieces of stem.

Echeveria

Lots of different varieties of these, almost all with fascinating leaf colouring and regular summer flowers. A windowsill filled with flowering echeverias presents an unbelieveable range of colours. Keep water off the leaves and they are little bother.

Echinocereus grusonii
Barrel cactus
The round barrel cactus with prominent yellow spines is one of the most splendid of all plants. Quite the pride of my small collection, it has grown at twice the pace of the other plants, yet has no special attention. A must in any cactus collection.

Epiphyllum

There are many hybrids of these succulent plants with large spatula-shaped leaves and flowers of unimaginable colour and brilliance. Needs slightly richer, moisture-holding compost, but tolerates very variable conditions with no marked ill effects.

Euphorbia splendens
Crown of thorns
This is the very spiteful crown of thorns (a jab from the thorns produces a nasty rash) and has small but brilliantly coloured red flowers. It will grow anywhere in reasonable light and temperature. Cuttings, allowed to dry for a day before inserting, will root readily in warm temperature of around 18°C (65°F). A careful watch should be kept for troublesome mealy bug on older plants.

Overleaf A variety of plants creates a happy working environment
1   *Neanthe bella*
2   *Adiantum cuneatum*
3   *Scindapsus aureus*
4   *Howeia forsteriana*
5   *Rhoicissus rhomboidea*
6   *Philodendron scandens*
7   *Ceropegia woodii*
8   *Billbergia windii*
9   Saintpaulia
10   *Sansevieria trifasciata laurentii*

Kalanchoe daigremontiana

At one time known as bryophyllum, the principal fascination of this plant is the way in which completely formed plantlets develop along the edge of the leaf. These root easily in almost any growing medium, and new plants will grow like a weed.

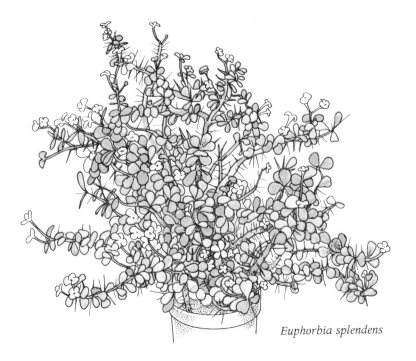

Euphorbia splendens

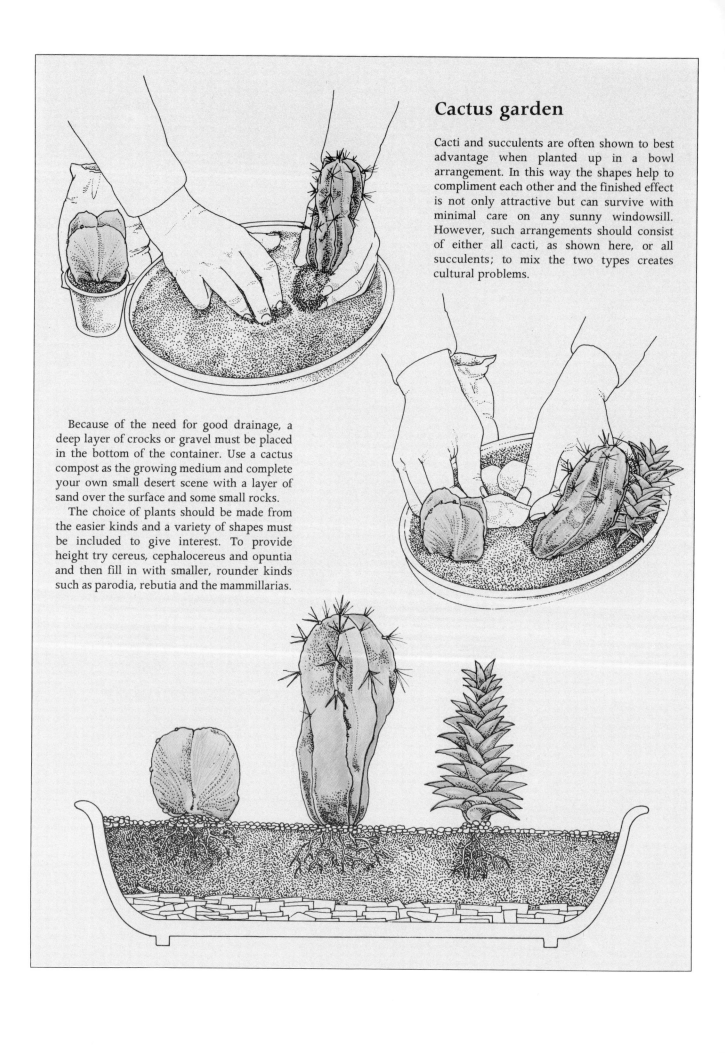

Cactus garden

Cacti and succulents are often shown to best advantage when planted up in a bowl arrangement. In this way the shapes help to compliment each other and the finished effect is not only attractive but can survive with minimal care on any sunny windowsill. However, such arrangements should consist of either all cacti, as shown here, or all succulents; to mix the two types creates cultural problems.

Because of the need for good drainage, a deep layer of crocks or gravel must be placed in the bottom of the container. Use a cactus compost as the growing medium and complete your own small desert scene with a layer of sand over the surface and some small rocks.

The choice of plants should be made from the easier kinds and a variety of shapes must be included to give interest. To provide height try cereus, cephalocereus and opuntia and then fill in with smaller, rounder kinds such as parodia, rebutia and the mammillarias.

Lithops
Living stones
On close inspection these will be found to be quite varied in shape and colour, but they all resemble small stones or pebbles, hence the common name of living stones. Can be raised from seed which is very expensive, so every care should be exercised when sowing and a constant temperature of around 21°C (70°F) should be provided. These are always seen at their best as a collection in a shallow pan.

Mammillaria
No collection of cacti could possibly be gathered without including these lovely barrel-shaped plants in their neat, symmetrical forms. *Mammillaria rhodantha* has lovely spines and produces tiny red flowers in the summer. My *M. hahniana* has the appearance of a ball of grey wool as a result of natural straggling hairs that completely obscure the plant. *Mammillaria elongata* has an attractive tubular body, is an overall dull yellow in colour and forms a neat cluster.

Notocactus leninghausii
Develops into a tallish cylinder of sulphur yellow growth that is lopsided at the top, which adds considerably to the attraction of the plant. Slow to mature, but age greatly enhances the appearance of this fine plant. Does not normally flower in its early years but well worth having, nevertheless.

Opuntia
Prickly pear
The prickly pears are among the best known of all, and have pads of growth that are viciously spined, or have countless bristles that stick into everything and anything that comes into contact with them.

Dark green pads of *O. leucotricha* carry the most incredible armoury of spines, but if one remembers to handle it with care, it develops into a magnificent plant. The varieties of *O. microdasys* have bristles rather than barbs but also require care when handling. Almost all are easily managed and root readily from pads removed and treated as cuttings.

Parodia
These are rewarding plants that are easily raised from seed, hence the many varieties available. All will flower freely over a long period, and have the added benefit of coming into flower at a very early age. Ideal for restricted space, as the compact rounded shapes take up little room. A collection of these small plants makes an ideal display for a sunny windowsill.

Rebutia
For the average grower of cacti on the windowsill the many hybridised kinds of these could well prove to be the most appealing of all. Because of their neat round shape and clustering habit they require little space, and can be almost guaranteed to produce flowers. Can be raised from seed, or by peeling off offsets and rooting them individually.

Schlumbergera gaertnerii
Easter or Whitsun cactus
Produced in vast quantities as a flowering pot plant, these are better known as Whitsun or Easter cactus, and need good light to do well. Once in flower the plant should remain in a light window position, and they will benefit from being placed out of doors during the summer months in a sheltered, sunny location. Cuttings of individual, or two-pad leaf sections will root readily. Keep moist and feed them with weak liquid fertiliser once established.

Zygocactus truncatus
Christmas cactus
Very similar in appearance to the foregoing, this one has the common name of Christmas cactus simply because it flowers at that particular time of year. Plants should never be allowed to become bone dry, but the soil should never become saturated.

Three cacti – opuntia, Cephalocereus senilis and rebutia

Bulbs can always be relied upon to provide a cheerful display of flowers
Top left Hippeastrum, sometimes known as amaryllis
Top right *Clivia nobilis*
Left A colourful spring display of irises and crocuses
Right The ever popular hyacinth, grown for its heady scent as well as its attractive flowers

CHAPTER 10
Bulbs, corms and rhizomes

*O*ne of the cheeriest sights of spring is a golden bed of daffodils swaying gently in the breeze. Their vibrant colour lifts the doldrums of winter and heralds the new growth of the year. Lately, many people have been discovering that a breath of spring can be enjoyed before the onset of the actual season by planting up containers of bulbs to flower indoors during late winter.

Most bulbs are suitable for indoor growing, hyacinths, popular for their heady scent, being the most familiar. When buying the bulbs it is very important that they should be in prime condition. Look for signs of eelworm and don't bother with dried-up specimens. Many garden centres supply bulbs which have been specially prepared for early forcing, again hyacinths are the most common, being prepared to flower at Christmas. If, however, you see the bulbs on sale before the middle of August, you can be sure that they will not have had the time to be properly prepared and will not flower as expected.

Potting

Bulbs for indoor growing should be potted sometime in late summer (August–September). Use a large shallow container rather than the conventional pot; do try to use one that has drainage holes. If this is not possible, put a layer of gravel mixed with charcoal in the bottom of the container; charcoal will help to keep the soil sweet.

When planting, specially prepared bulb fibre is the usual recommendation, but I find that my own bulbs respond very well to potting in John Innes No. 2 with a little peat added.

Fill the bottom of the container with compost and then put in the bulbs, placing them close together – nothing looks worse than a few lonely 'daffs' sticking up out of a vast container. By planting the container with a number of bulbs placed at two different levels you can achieve a colourful massed display.

Wrap the containers in large black refuse bags or similar and store them in a cool dark place for at least 10 weeks, or until you see the first signs of growth.

When the shoots are about 2.5 cm (1 in) tall, bring the bulbs into the warmth. Do not put them in direct sun (although they do like a light position) and keep them moist.

Types

Clivia
Not strictly speaking a bulb, this plant has a thick, fleshy base to its stem. It needs a minimum temperature of around 16°C (60°F). Very durable with glossy strap-like leaves and bearing clusters of orange flowers on stout stems. Put in a reasonably light position and water regularly, feeding when established. John Innes No. 3 required when potting on.

Crocus
Use shallow bowls with drainage holes, and cover the holes with crocks before half filling with compost. Press bulbs almost touching into compost then cover with soil. After flowering, let the leaves die back, dry off the soil and then plant the bulbs in the garden.

Gloriosa rothschildiana
Tender subjects that should be planted several to a large pot filled with John Innes No. 3 to which extra peat has been added. These are best started in a warm greenhouse and will require several canes at least a yard long to support this normally quick growing plant. The brightly coloured scarlet flowers appear in summer. Place in good light, but not strong sun and keep moist. Dies down in winter, when the tubers should be kept warm and dry.

Planting bulbs

Many types of bulbs can be grown in bowls indoors to create a colourful spring display e.g. narcissi, tulips, hyacinths, crocuses, snowdrops and grape hyacinths.

Bulbs can be planted close together (but not touching) in a single layer or, for a fuller display, can be layer-planted. The diagram shows the two layers correctly placed so that the lower bulbs can grow up through the spaces left between the bulbs in the upper layer.

After planting, the bulbs should be plunged outside in a garden frame until growth starts (about 10 weeks). If a frame is not available wrap the containers in black polythene and store in a cool place such as a garage or garden shed.

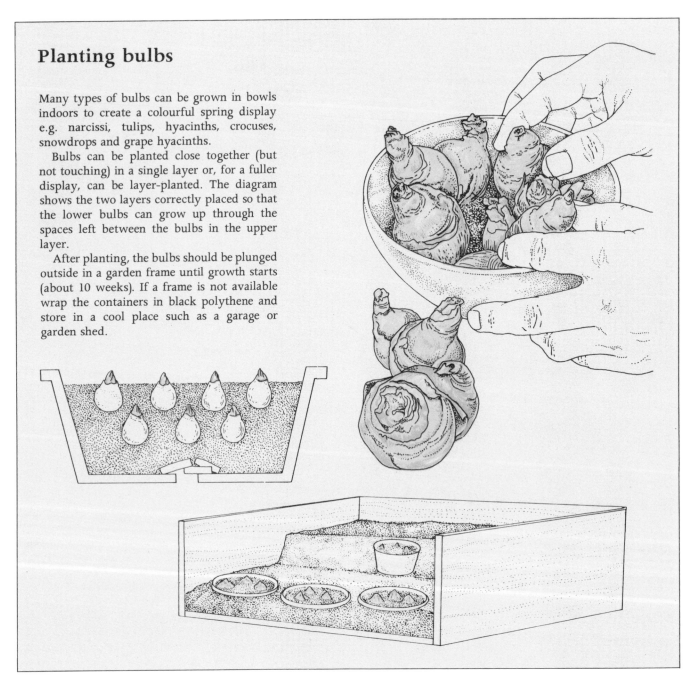

Haemanthus

Odd is a suitable word to describe these bulbous plants with their broad strap leaves that are very short. In time they will produce a peculiar white, red or orange flower that resembles a somewhat ragged shaving brush! Best planted in early spring with the tip of the bulb just showing above the soil. If kept warm and almost dry in winter it is no trouble to care for.

Hippeastrum

Expensive, large bulbous plants with strap leaves and extremely exotic trumpet-shaped flowers that stand proudly on stems which may attain a height of a yard or more. After flowering in early spring keep the plant watered and fed and place out of doors in a sunny position during the summer. Take care that watering and feeding are not neglected during this period. As the end of summer approaches, allow the plant to dry out and then store it in a warm spot in autumn. Then pre-heat the bulb in warm water before starting into growth again at the end of the year. For success all that is necessary is to purchase good quality bulbs and provide warmth, light and moisture.

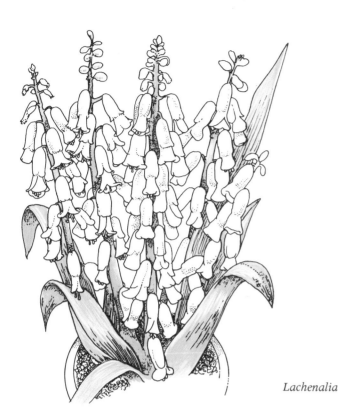

Lachenalia

Lachenalia
Another tender bulb originating from South Africa and commonly named Cape cowslip. Growth is from September to June when flowers of orange-yellow colouring appear. Six to eight bulbs in a hanging basket produce a good display, and they should be brought in to the warmth in September to start into growth. After flowering keep bone dry and place out of doors in full sun.

Lilies
There are many of these to choose from, some needing different types of soil in respect of acidity, so information must be sought from the supplier when the bulbs are purchased. Information on culture varies, but I find bulbs purchased and potted in mid-winter (January–February) will flower perfectly during the summer. Buy the shorter varieties for preference. Offer cool conditions after potting. Keep compost moist and put in a lightly shaded spot and a fine display of colour will result.

Narcissus
There are many varieties to choose from some scented, double-flowered or dwarf and a really grand display can be made as follows: fill an 8 in pot, that has been crocked to about half its depth, with John Innes No. 3, put in a layer of bulbs and cover them with soil. Then place another layer of bulbs on the layer of soil before filling the pot to just below its rim with compost. Try not to overlap the bulbs. The double layer will ensure a superb display when flowers appear.

Nerine
Hardy South African bulbs that are kept dry and dormant during the summer months, preferably on a greenhouse shelf in full sun. Sun baking will encourage the flowers which are carried on 45 cm (18 in) stems and are mainly in pink shades. Indoors they should have good light and be allowed to dry out between each watering.

Tulip
Pot in September, using John Innes No. 3. Once indoors, water freely and place pot in a light position. Shorter stemmed varieties are more suitable for indoor decoration.

Zantedeschia

Zantedeschia
The arum lily, *Z. aethiopica*, is not everyone's cup of tea as an indoor plant, but it grows well enough and produces spectacular white flowers if kept moist and well fed, and given reasonable light. Less water and feeding is required in winter, and during summer months the plants can be placed out of doors. When potting on use John Innes No. 3 and pot firmly.

CHAPTER 11
Bottle gardens

Bottle gardens are adaptations of the Wardian case principle of keeping tender, moisture-loving plants in an environment that would otherwise be difficult to simulate in the average living room. Dr Ward, after whom Wardian cases are named, was a keen plantsman who discovered that tender ferns lived for many years, virtually without attention, in the atmosphere of his ingenious cases, which were first used in about 1830.

When cases are hermetically sealed, watering is unnecessary, as moisture transpiring from the plants' leaves condenses on the inside of the glass container, and eventually finds its way back into the soil. Completely sealed containers are, however, less attractive than those with a small opening because the film of moisture which forms on the inside of the glass obscures the plants from view. Bottle gardens with open tops will require a little water very occasionally, when the plants are seen to be flagging, or when the soil surface is obviously dry. Trickle the water gently on to the soil surface by means of a flexible rubber hose pipe (the one from the washing machine is ideal).

Disused carboys make excellent bottle gardens, as they are spacious inside and permit the use of slightly taller plants, though sweet bottles and clear glass jars of various kinds may also be used for smaller, or even individual, plants. Almost the first step on acquiring a carboy will be the need to give it a thorough cleaning with detergent, both inside and out, in order to remove stains and any harmful residue. Be warned, however, that the use of hot water is positively not advised, because of the risk of cracking the glass.

For my money, the best bottle garden of all is in fact a disused fish tank – these are roomier, more accessible, and much more attractive when plants have been established.

A further benefit is that the fish tank will almost surely have its own built-in strip light. Presence of soft lighting will greatly enhance the appearance of the plants, and the gentle warmth that is given off will considerably improve plant growth. Not that one wants plants to grow too quickly, but it is more agreeable to watch them prosper rather than shrivel and die.

When planting the fish tank one should apply the same principle as for the bottle garden – you require about a 6-in depth of compost that has had some charcoal worked into it to prevent it becoming sour. The compost should be laid over a bed of gravel which will collect surplus water. A pleasing contoured effect can be achieved on the surface of the compost by putting in stones or pieces of bark before introducing the plants. If the tank is large enough you could scatter pebbles on the surface of the compost to give the appearance of a path.

The object should be to design and plant up a miniature garden, using tall, medium and creeping plants with stones and so on setting them off as one would expect in a well arranged garden, rather than to just fill the tank with lots of different plants!

Another advantage is that a fish tank does not place so many restrictions on choice of plants as does the conventional bottle garden – somewhat larger plants can be used, as their encroachment on other plants can be simply remedied by means of pruning.

Plants to choose
Next, and most important, is the choice of plants. Here it must be emphasised that only slow-growing plants should be used. See the list at the end of the chapter for an idea of suitable plants. A florist friend informs me that his charge for dismantling overgrown carboys is more than his charge for arranging

plants initially – so beware. The same friend illustrated his point when he showed me a carboy that had been planted up less than one year previously with the apparently harmless dead nettle, *Gynura sarmentosa*. In a matter of months the plant had filled all the available space in the carboy and had a few shoots inspecting the prospects outside the bottle!

Plants to avoid

The use of flowering plants presents problems, for when flowers fade and die they become vulnerable to fungus diseases, which will quickly spread to other plants in the container if left unchecked. Having warned against the use of flowering plants, I can see in my mind's eye an established bottle garden in perfect condition, in the centre of which nestled an African violet in full flower and obviously not in the least concerned about having been an 'intruder' for the previous two years. In general, however, though you may be tempted to experiment, it is better to concentrate on foliage plants when making your selection.

Purchased plants ought to be in pots no larger than 3 in in diameter if they are to pass conveniently through the neck of the bottle. Plants in larger pots, besides being too tall or spreading in themselves, suffer considerably from having their roots damaged in the planting process. Also, care must be taken to choose plants with flexible leaves that will bend easily as they are lowered into the bottle.

The planting operation

Before planting begins the following materials should be at hand: sufficient pebbles $\frac{3}{8}$ in in size (ballast from your local builders' merchant, is ideal) to provide a 2-in layer in the bottom of the bottle (these should be thoroughly wetted before putting in position); a small amount of charcoal (from any gardening shop) for mixing with the compost to prevent it becoming sour too quickly. Sour soil inevitably results in the formation of an unsightly coating of algae on the surface of the compost. Large carboys will need about a 5-in layer of compost, which should be of an open texture. John Innes No. 2 potting compost would be a suitable medium with the addition of two handfuls of sharp grit to improve drainage.

Use a funnel, shaped from a piece of cardboard, to pour the materials through the narrow neck of the bottle and into the desired position.

Simple tools as planting and cultural aids

Some simple tools will be needed for planting, pruning and cleaning. Mine are nothing more than a few 2 ft canes, to the ends of which I tie a teaspoon (as substitute for a trowel), a table fork (for a rake), and an old cotton reel wedged

1. *No special equipment is required to start a bottle garden. The tools are merely ordinary household items tied firmly to strong canes*

1

onto the end of a cane, which is used for firming the soil around the roots after planting. For pruning, my favourite tool is a razor blade secured into a cleft in the end of a cane. For a scavenging tool I follow in the steps of the park keeper and tie a nail to the end of a cane; this is used for spearing yellow leaves and severed pieces that the pruner has dealt with.

A trial run
To obviate the need for difficult manoeuvring of plants in the confined space of the containers it is better to do a mock-up outside the bottle first, in order to achieve the desired effect. Do this by preparing a bed of compost of approximately the same dimensions as the surface of the soil in the container, and on this

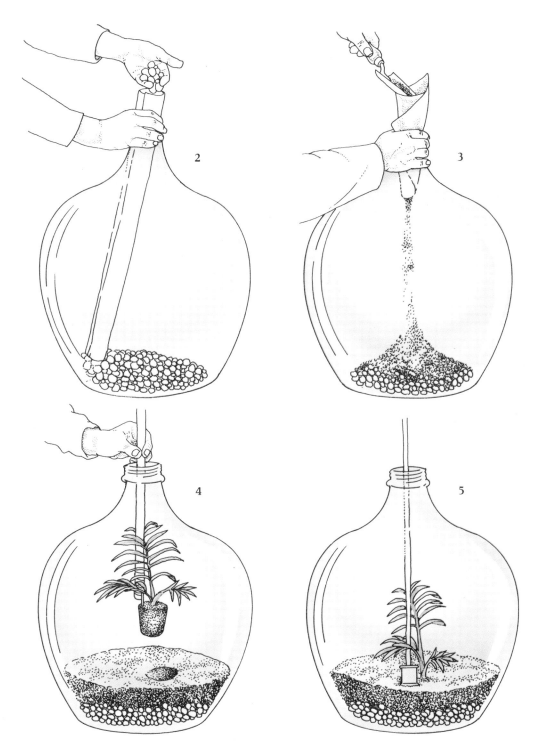

2. *An even layer of small pebbles is introduced to the carboy by means of a cardboard tube*
3. *The potting compost is the next layer to go in through a paper funnel*
4. *The plants can be manoeuvred into position by placing a spiked stick firmly through the rootball*
5. *The planting operation is completed by using a cotton reel to firm the plants in*

*A finished bottle garden
planted up with a selection
of small delicate plants*

arrange the plants to your satisfaction; it is then an easy matter to place them accordingly in the bottle. The standard carboy will accommodate five or six small plants; if more than this number are planted they will quickly become congested.

Positioning the plants
Great care will be needed when the actual planting operation takes place. Although it may appear harsh, I find that using my park keeper's prodder to spear through the root ball is the simplest way of inserting plants and manoeuvring them into position. One of the other tools can then be used to hold the plant firm while the prodder is withdrawn. I often feel that the dextrous use of elongated chopsticks would be the perfect answer to planting. Or, as an acquaintance once suggested, bottle

gardens should be fitted with zip fasteners! Dr Ward would seem to have had the ideal answer when he fitted a door in the side of his more ornamental Wardian cases.

In common with the majority of foliage plants, your carboy will require a light position and protection from strong sunlight. Ornamentation in the way of stones, bark, twigs, wee men and such like is purely a matter of personal taste. These can be used to good effect if they are placed with care and used sparingly.

Suitable plants

Acorus gramineus variegatus Erect golden grass.

Adiantum cuneatum The delicately-leaved maidenhair fern.

Asplenium nidus Only for larger bottles, as eventually the plant becomes rather large.

Begonia boweri This plant will pay for the bother of finding a supplier.

Begonia Cleopatra Makes neat hummocks of dull green and bronze-coloured foliage, with the prospect of pale pink flowers coming as a bonus.

Begonia rex Only the smaller-leaved sorts. There is a danger of mildew attacking the leaves of these plants in close, damp conditions.

Cocos weddelliana Fine feathery fern that can be utilised as a background plant for the arrangement. When too large, it can be removed and potted into a conventional container.

Codiaeums (crotons) Many of these develop into very substantial plants, often outgrowing the small greenhouse, let alone the bottle garden – so select with care.

Codiaeum pictum and C. Apple Leaf Both Codiaeum pictum and the variety Apple Leaf will remain reasonably small, though their colouring, yellow and green, is rather dull when compared with the rainbow colours of most codiaeums.

Cryptanthuses In many varieties – choose those with smaller leaves and more compact rosettes.

Dracaena godseffiana Florida Beauty See description on page 71.

Dracaena Rededge With a combination of dull green and equally dull red foliage, this is another plant that will form a pleasing background.

Dracaena sanderiana Becomes tall in time, but useful for providing a little height in the centre of the arrangement.

Episcia There are a number of these that will be admirably suited, as they are mostly compact and will enjoy the warm and close conditions.

Euonymus japonicus aureopictus A hardy ourdoor plant with attractive golden foliage that can be pruned to shape at any time.

Ficus pumila A quick grower, but regular pruning will keep it in check.

Ficus radicans With attractive pale green and white variegation, this plant will appreciate the close and warm conditions of a bottle garden.

Fittonia argyroneura The dwarf miniature form of this plant is probably a better choice, but either will be well suited to the humid and warm conditions. This dwarf variety is commonly known as little snakeskin plant on account of its leaf markings.

Fittonia verschaffeltii See description on page 73.

Hederas (ivies) Select the small-leaved variegated ones and cut them back when they spread too far.

Hoya carnosa variegata Easily checked by pruning if it becomes too invasive. Can either be used as a ground-cover plant or be tied to a short cane to give a little extra height in an arrangement.

Maranta leuconeura erythrophylla A fine plant capable of being a feature if planted by itself in the bottle garden, with only the odd bit of ivy or *Ficus pumila* to act as a foil.

Maranta l. kerchoveana Only for larger containers.

Neanthe bella A trouble-free miniature palm.

Peperomias *Peperomia magnoliaefolia, P. hederaefolia* and *P. caperata*. The last two form large clumps that will be difficult to prune, so use them only in more spacious bottle gardens.

Pteris cretica One of the many smaller ferns that are perfect for this purpose.

Saintpaulia In their many fine colours, these will give a lot of pleasure in the fish tank where it will be possible to remove dead flowers without difficulty.

Sansevieria hahnii variegata Expensive and scarce.

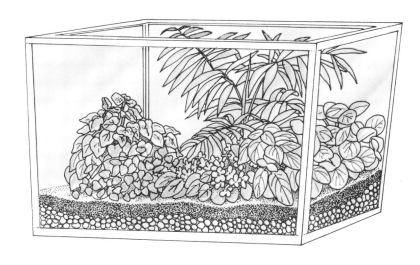

Sansevieria trifasciata laurentii Not one of the best, but it offers a pleasing change of leaf shape.

Selaginella Makes clumps of mossy green foliage which are perfect for the bottle garden.

Tillandsia Compact bromeliads in many varieties. *T. cyanea* is one of the best if there is a choice.

Tradescantias Many kinds, some rather invasive, but even those can be pruned if in a fish tank.

An old fish tank is much easier to plant up and care for than the traditional carboy

Ficus pumila and pteris are two excellent small-scale plants suitable for bottle garden arrangements

CHAPTER 12
Plants for the office

The growth and popularity of houseplants has been something quite remarkable in itself, and it would seem even more remarkable that following on to their popularity in the home, there has been created a desire for plants among people at their places of work. In the hotel foyer or restaurant this is quite understandable, but it is remarkable that the interior of many offices have almost become miniature botanic gardens.

The office windowsill plant is still very much in evidence, but such plants have now given way to much bolder schemes whereby entire floors of offices are planned with as much emphasis placed on the location of plants as there is on the desks that at first sight would appear to be more important.

Although we may refer to them as office plants they are, in fact, no different from the general range of houseplants now available. In many cases they are, however, subject to much harsher treatment than their counterparts in the living room window. Where the home gardener will purchase a plant with the express intention of giving it every possible care, Mabel in the office receives it as a birthday gift from her colleagues and looks at it with bewilderment, wondering what on earth she is going to do with it. Generally speaking, given a week or two of the inexperienced, and not always interested, care of Mabel, and there is no doubt what should be done with it!

Most plantings are confined to large containers with a selection of plants that are either growing conventionally in soil or, as has been the trend in recent years, they are growing in a mixture of water and nutrients with plants being anchored by pebbles of some kind. There are a number of different systems whereby plants can be grown very successfully in this way.

The plants will, in most instances, have been installed by a plantsman specialising in this field and this person will usually be responsible for the maintenance of the plants in the office, ensuring that they are watered, fed and so on. It is usual for the company owning the offices to enter into a contract with the plant supplier, in which case you usually require the latter to replace any plants that may be ailing. Such an arrangement is usually much more satisfactory than simply allowing any person in the office who is available to care for the plants.

Even the supplier will make stipulations when plants are being considered as a possibility for any particular office. Besides a minimum year round temperature in the region of 16°C (60°F), the most important need will be adequate light to enable plants to grow. The average office, well lit with banks of fluorescent lighting and evenly controlled atmosphere and temperature will be about right.

Plants in dark corners simply will not do well unless special lighting is installed above the plant display; there are pendant lights made especially for this purpose. These lights are suspended about 4 ft above the plant and possess qualities that, as far as the plants' requirements are concerned, are not dissimilar to natural daylight. If spotlights are to be used to highlight the beauty of the plants, these should be placed considerably further away, otherwise the plant foliage may be scorched.

The problems

There are several problems to be overcome if office plants are to survive: excessive heat, dry atmosphere, inattention at week-ends and lack of any sort of facility for performing so much as the simplest potting operation, to name but a few. Plants will probably have to suffer high temperatures, though following the advice given in the chapter on routine culture will help to relieve the harmful effects of the dry atmosphere. Lack of attention at week-ends may be overcome to some extent by purchasing plants in pots of reasonable size; such plants will be better able to stand several consecutive days without attention. The soil in small 'tots' or 'thumb' pots soon lacks nutriment, and dries at an alarming rate when plants are stood for any length of time on a sunny windowledge.

Lack of attention at week-ends
Brief respite from watering and general care is a blessing for the plant that is treated like an only child and is provided with all the attention that this book describes, plus a little more for good measure. But, for the office plant that often has its share of neglect during the week, a good baking on the window-ledge in dry soil at week-ends can prove fatal. So, have a care, and move plants into a shaded corner on Friday evenings where they will be much happier over Saturday and Sunday.

Rarely can the need for adequate light be overstressed if plants are to succeed, but equal emphasis must be placed on their need for protection from strong sunshine. In the modern office block consisting of concrete and acres of glass, plants will have ample light in almost any position. Morning and evening sun is comparatively harmless, but mid-day sun, magnified by the glass, will quickly reduce indoor plants to a few dry, shrivelled leaves. Some plants appear to tolerate these Sahara-like conditions reasonably well, but even they would benefit from some protection. Among the few in this category are chlorophytum, tradescantia, sansevieria, impatiens (sometimes growing astonishingly well), ivies and the occasional kangaroo vine (*Cissus antarctica*), though the last-mentioned is inclined to become very hard and yellow in appearance eventually. Perhaps the main reason for ivies, chlorophytum, and trade-scantia being so prevalent is their ease of propagation, which ensures an ample supply.

The radiator problem
Office radiators present a further problem, as these are frequently placed along the wall immediately under windows. This is ideal for office staff on a cold winter's morning, but death to any plants in the direct stream of hot air on the windowledge above. Should there be no alternative to the window position above the radiator, care must be taken to increase the width of the shelf with a piece of hardboard or similar material – hot air will then be directed above the plants and not through their leaves. Where radiators are fitted in the home, this precaution also applies.

Suitable plants for the office

Aspidistra lurida (cast iron plant)	Light, shady position. Minimum temperature 13°C (55°F)
Cacti and other succulents	Good light. Minimum temperature 10°C (50°F)
Chlorophytum (spider plant)	Good light. Minimum temperature 7°C (45°F)
Cissus antarctica (kangaroo vine)	Shady position. Temperature required: 10° to 18°C (50° to 65°F)
Coleus	Good light. Minimum temperature 16°C (60°F)
Euonymus japonicus aureovariegatus (golden bush)	Likes cool conditions but plenty of light. Hardy shrub
Fatshedera lizei	Reasonable light. Minimum temperature 10°C (50°F)
Ficus elastica (rubber plant)	Good light but not full sunlight. Minimum temperature 13°C (55°F)
Heptapleurum	Light shade. Minimum temperature 7°C (45°F)
Impatiens (busy lizzie)	Good light. Minimum temperature 13°C (55°F)
Kentia (palm)	Good light with shade from strong sunlight. Minimum temperature 18°C (65°F)
Monstera (Swiss cheese plant)	Light shade. Minimum temperature 16°C (60°F)
Philodendron scandens (sweetheart vine)	Light shade. Minimum temperature 16°C (60°F)
Sansevieria trifasciata laurentii (mother-in-law's tongue)	Good light. Minimum temperature 10°C (50°F)
Schefflera (umbrella plant)	Light shade. Minimum temperature 13°C (55°F)
Tradescantia (wandering Jew)	Good light but avoid strong sunlight. Minimum temperature 7°C (45°F)

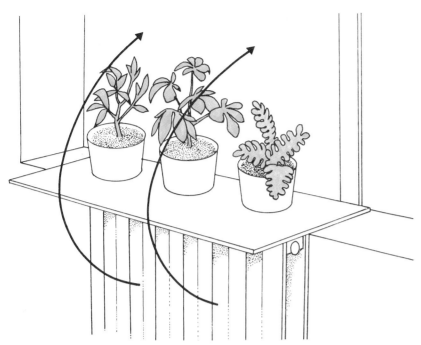

Hot air from a radiator may be deflected over the plants on the windowsill by placing them on a piece of hardboard. This tip can, of course, be used in the home as well as the office

An interesting trial

Although we are continually being reminded of the need for potting plants on into larger containers when it becomes necessary, astonishing results can also be achieved by regular feeding. On record there is proof of an interesting trial that may help to prove the point. By way of experiment, a rubber plant (*Ficus elastica*) was taken direct from a peat cutting bed and 'potted' into Sorbo rubber material fashioned in the shape of a pot. A deep slit was made in the rubber, into which the cutting was inserted, and the 'rubber pot ball' was then snugly fitted into a 5-in pot. In the space of three years the rubber plant in rubber 'soil' grew to a height of 30 in and had 20 firm leaves. The leaves were slightly smaller than those of plants grown in ordinary compost, though it is interesting to note that no leaves were shed during this period. Similar experiments, equally successful, were carried out with bromeliads and *Begonia masoniana*. 'Compost' of this kind, because of the slower rate of growth of the plant and the extra attention required, is not a commercial proposition, but it did prove that the potting medium is not quite the important factor that it would appear to be. I mention the experiment purely as a matter of interest, and would not expect plants to prosper under normal room or office conditions unless they were potted in a suitable compost. Compared to other plants, those in the Sorbo rubber required more frequent watering, though there was the advantage that the water drained away rapidly, thus preventing waterlogging. No extra feeding was required.

Holiday periods

In the course of time the observant plant owner gets to know almost the exact requirements of particular plants in respect of watering and feeding. During holiday periods, such information can be a considerable asset, as one can give precise instructions to the person entrusted with the care of plants during one's absence. The inexperienced person, having the misguided impression that too much is better than too little, is almost invariably tempted to over-water and over-feed plants left in his or her care. In respect of plant care, there is no doubt whatsoever that too many cooks spoil the broth, so, when absent from the office for any length of time, select one person to administer to the needs of your plants, and give precise instructions concerning the amount and frequency of both watering and feeding.

Feeding

As already mentioned, another drawback is lack of facilities for carrying out simple potting operations. The office manager may considerately fail to notice a few clean plants in clean containers standing in saucers and ashtrays, but the line is firmly drawn when sacks of John Innes potting compost appear in the 'typing pool'. Therefore, if potting on is out of the question, the need for regular and adequate feeding is doubly important. As indoor plant fertilisers are all packed in neat boxes or bottles these days, there should be no objection to their presence among the paper clips.

CHAPTER 13
Plant hygiene

Standing your plants outside in the rain, is often mentioned as being a simple way of cleaning plant leaves. Perhaps the lady who wrote to me from Burnley in February and complained that her rubber plant was looking decidedly sad following its recent spell in the rain-drenched garden had done just this. Possibly a warm gentle summer rain is harmless but here it would be wise to compare plants with human beings, and one shudders to think of standing unprotected in a Lancashire garden in mid-February!

Plants with leaves of a rough or hairy texture will be damaged if cleaned with a sponge or cloth. Many such plants, *Peperomia caperata* for example, can be cleaned of dust by placing your hand over the top of the pot and inverting the plant in a bucketful of tepid water. Gently move the plant to and fro through the water, and this will remove all loose dust and greatly improve the appearance of the plant. Hairy-leaved plants, such as saintpaulias, can have dust removed by using a soft camel hair brush.

For all other plants, proprietary leaf cleaning preparations are available, and reasonably good results may also be achieved by using a mixture of equal parts of milk and water, or neat brown ale. One of the white-oil insecticides will also improve the appearance of plants if used at a strength of one dessertspoonful to one gallon of water. Liquid paraffin (not paraffin-oil) weakly diluted in water is also suitable for tougher-leaved subjects. Oil preparations give an unnatural appearance to leaves if used at an excessive strength, and will have a tendency to turn the edges of leaves brown if used too frequently. Actual cleaning of leaves in the average home need only be done every six to eight weeks, although plants with larger leaves benefit from regular dusting. Some of the aerosol sprays are excellent for cleaning the leaves of shiny-leaved foliage plants, such as monsteras, rubber plants and glossy-leaved philodendrons. But there are a few precautions that one should take, and the most important of these is never to use cleaning chemicals on leaves that are exposed to direct sunlight. Equally important, plants that have been cleaned with any form of chemical should not be subjected to low temperature until the effects of the chemical have worn off.

Drastic treatment

My local railway station generally displays a reasonable collection of foliage plants that are lovingly tended by a semi-retired member of the staff. Summoned by an urgent message from the gardener one spring morning, we arrived at the station to inspect his fly- and dust-ridden ivies, some of which had trails almost 6 ft in length. The man whose charge they were, looked on with some concern when buckets were produced, malathion solution prepared, and his plants unceremoniously plunged in the mixture and given a good scrub. All dead leaves, greenfly, dust and a few sound leaves were removed in the process, but the treatment certainly did them a power of good.

The 'spring clean'

Such treatment would be a trifle harsh for the less dusty plants growing indoors; nevertheless, it is wise to give them a good spring clean to set them on their feet for the new season. Insert new stakes where necessary, remove dead leaves and pot on any plants that may be in need of a larger container. Although potting on may not be necessary, almost all plants will benefit from having the top inch or so of soil removed and replaced with fresh compost.

Use a pointed stick (a pencil is ideal) to disturb and remove the old soil, being careful not to probe too deeply.

Recommended insecticides

Malathion and liquid derris are two insecticides that can be safely used on the majority of indoor plants to control pests, provided the manufacturers' instructions are carefully followed. Take the precaution of wearing rubber gloves, and treat plants outside to avoid unpleasant smells indoors. Smaller, and trailing plants that will fit into a bucket are best treated by immersing them in the solution you intend to use. Larger plants should be drenched with the insecticide by spraying it on, using a small hand spray and paying particular attention to the underside of the leaves where most pests make their home.

Besides leaf cleaners, there are all sorts of other chemicals that, for convenience, are contained in aerosols. Many of these can be lethal as far as the average indoor plant is concerned, and plants should, therefore, be kept well out of the way when they are being used. Aerosols in general use such as hairsprays, furniture polish and fly-killers can be damaging to plants indoors. Plant insecticides are now available in aerosol form and they are very easy to use making it possible to treat both sides of leaves effectively. For the person with a small collection of indoor plants these sprays are by the far the cleanest, safest and most effective. But, as with all chemicals and fertilisers used in connection with potted plants, be they in the home or in the greenhouse, one should use discretion and never be tempted to apply them too frequently, or in contradiction to the manufacturers' recommendations.

Besides more conventional insecticides there are systemic kinds that, as the name implies, are taken in through the system of the plant, so that insects that survive by sucking the sap are destroyed. These are usually made-up in a liquid solution which is watered into the soil around the plant. Again, for the safety of you and your plants, be sure to follow the manufacturer's instructions.

The pests

The following list describes some of the pests you are most likely to encounter on houseplants and describes the symptoms of their presence and the best way of treating an attack.

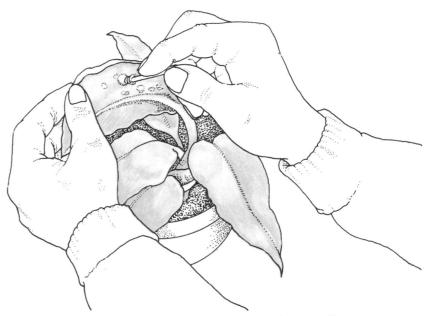

The most effective way to get rid of mealy bugs is to dab them individually with methylated spirit

Mealy bug

Mealy bugs are one of the more easily detected pests, being white in colour and resembling small woodlice in appearance. Making contact with the young mealy bugs, which are protected by a cotton-wool-like covering, presents a problem when spraying. It can be overcome by dabbing them with a piece of cotton wool (tied to the end of a match stick) that has been soaked in methylated spirits.

Red spider

Red spider mite, much smaller than the mealy bug, is difficult to see with the naked eye, and its presence is often only detected when leaves become brown around the edges and take on a generally dry appearance. Plants badly infested will eventually have small webs on the undersides of the leaves. However, they may be detected earlier when tiny pin-prick holes appear on the underside of the leaves, or by using a magnifying glass to see them busily going about their business of slowly sucking the life out of your plant. The perfect breeding ground for red spiders is a plant kept in hot, dry conditions; so, where possible, frequent spraying of the foliage with water will help to deter them.

Other mites

Perhaps the most damaging pests of all are the almost invisible mites, though fortunately they are less common these days. They seem to have a particular attraction for the ivies and African violets. Their trade mark is hard and distorted pit-marked foliage, badly infested ivies being eventually reduced to leafless stalks. Unfortunately, there is no simple cure that can be recommended for general use. Control can only be carried out swiftly and effectively in nursery conditions by using a highly toxic insecticide that has to be treated with the greatest respect. One can also exercise some control by cutting affected plants hard back to the point where they are almost devoid of leaves, in the hope that new growth, when produced, will be clear of mites. Should other plants in a collection be vulnerable, affected plants must be disposed of, preferably by burning.

Greenfly

Greenfly is sometimes troublesome, but simply erradicated, either by using one of the earlier mentioned products, or, more cheaply, by immersing the plants in soapy water. Larger plants can be sprayed with the same inexpensive solution.

Scale insects

The scale insects are hard-backed pests, coloured light brown when young and almost jet black when adult. These are predominant on the underside of the leaves, but are also to be seen on the stems. A sponge that has been soaked in malathion can be used to wipe them forcibly from where they are attached, remembering always to wear rubber gloves when handling insecticides. Scale insects that still persist may be removed with a well-directed thumb nail.

An important reminder

When using insecticides the maker's directions should be followed to the letter. If uncertain of your plant's reaction to a particular insecticide, it is advisable to experiment first by treating only one plant, or, if you have only one specimen of a particular plant, you should treat part of it in order to note the reaction.

Diseases and disorders

Symptoms	Possible cause	Treatment
Yellowing leaves	1 Old leaf	None required if it is one of the lower leaves that is affected.
	2 Too little light	Change position but avoid strong sunlight.
	3 Underfeeding	Feed during growing season with proprietary house plant food applied according to manufacturer's instructions. Repot.
	4 Sucking insect such as red spider mites	Improve humidity by spraying foliage regularly, spray with insecticide.
Variegated leaves loose colour	1 Too little light	Move nearer to source of light.
Leaf tips and margins go brown	1 Overwatering	Allow compost to dry out again before watering.
	2 Temperature too low	Move to a warmer room.
	3 Overfeeding	Check on amount and frequency of feeding and adjust if necessary. Do not feed when plant is not actively growing.
	4 Draughts	Move to draught-free position – not in line with windows and door.
	5 Lack of humidity	Take measures to increase humidity.
Brown or yellow spots on leaves	1 Sunscorch	Move plant away from strong direct sunlight. Do not leave water drops on leaves when watering.
	2 Draughts	Move to a draught-free position.
	3 Overwatering	Allow compost to dry out, take more care with watering.
	4 Overfeeding	Check on amount and frequency of feeding and adjust.
Leaf drop	1 Underwatering	Check plants regularly and water when compost is dry to the touch.
	2 Sudden changes in temperature	Avoid moving plants from room to room or place to place, especially in winter.
	3 Draughts	Avoid a position between door and windows.
Leaves and/or stems rotting	1 Overwatering	Reduce amount of water and do not allow water to remain on leaves or around base of stems.
Plants wilt	1 Too much heat	Move away from windowsill or heat source, watch watering.
	2 Underwatering	Give more water or water more frequently.
	3 Overwatering	May cause waterlogging of soil and kill roots. Allow compost to dry out before watering again.
Leggy growth	1 Too little light	Move nearer to a source of light.
No flowers on a plant which should flower	1 Too little light	Move nearer to a source of light.
	2 Temperature of room too high in evening	Move to a cooler position in evening but not into a draught.
	3 Plant too immature to flower	Wait.

CHAPTER 14
Simple propagation

Indoor plants can be increased by a variety of methods, seed sowing, leaf and stem cuttings, and division of plant clumps being the most practical. The nurseryman rarely resorts to the use of pips, date stones or pineapple tops in order to increase his stock, but a number of interesting plants can be produced in this way. Although increasing difficult plants that require constant high temperatures and high humidity may be out of the question, many of what one might call 'every-day plants' are comparatively easy to propagate.

Hygienic conditions

Hygienic conditions play an important part in successful propagation so pots, boxes, compost, and anything else that cuttings and seeds are likely to come into contact with, must be kept scrupulously clean. The propagating medium is equally important, so a potful of soil from the garden cannot be expected to give satisfactory results. One cannot go far wrong when using John Innes No. 1 potting compost, a soilless seed and cutting compost or clean moss peat with a little sharp sand added to it. Once rooted cuttings should be potted into a proper growing medium.

Pot sizes and cutting material

When starting smaller cuttings in pots, it will be found that the smaller pots, up to 3 in in diameter, give better results. Small cuttings inserted in large potfuls of compost rarely do well, as the medium tends to become sour long before the plant is able to establish itself. Tradescantias, and other plants that produce ample propagating material, do infinitely better if several pieces (up to seven) are put in one pot; these take on a mature appearance almost as soon as they have rooted. Rosette-forming plants do better when grown from individual pieces.

Simple propagating cases

An adequate temperature is a further pre-requisite of success. A constant temperature in the region of 18°C (65°F) is ideal for most subjects, and if the soil temperature can be maintained at the same level, then the need for 'green fingers' becomes relatively unimportant. Simple wooden propagating cases are easy to construct at home, and an ever-increasing range of models is on offer at almost any gardening shop. The majority of the latter are made of plastic and need little more than a supply of electricity for them to become operative. In these propagators, space is always at a premium, so it is wise to use shallow seed boxes for cuttings and for seeds in order to make maximum use of the available area. Light is of course essential for growth of cuttings and germinated seeds.

The polythene bag 'propagator'

Where one's purse, or need, does not extend to something as grand as a propagating case, reasonably good results may be obtained by covering cuttings with a polythene bag, or by placing both pot and cuttings in the bag and sealing the top. The object here is to reduce transpiration, thereby permitting leaves and stems to remain turgid while the rooting process takes place. Should there be no propagator, or polythene bag, cuttings will dry out and become limp, so lessening their chance of producing roots of their own.

Hormone rooting powder

Though by no means essential, the use of one of the proprietary hormone rooting powders will induce cuttings to root more readily, particularly if they have hard, woody stems. The severed ends of the cuttings should be moistened and then dipped in the rooting powder, before inserting them in the rooting medium.

To propagate tradescantia plants, take several healthy cuttings and insert them round the edge of a pot. These will soon root and form a new, attractive plant

Cuttings

The young gardener is forever being advised by the more experienced old hand that, when propagating, he must remember that the best new plants are almost invariably the result of using strong, unblemished material in the first place. This is indeed the case, and it goes without saying that the best propagator always accumulates the most rubbish. The important difference is that the efficient man can detect good from bad when preparing his cuttings, so he accumulates rubbish at his feet and not in his propagating beds. Though the greenhouse propagating bed containing thousands of cuttings may seem a far cry from the home-made propagator in the spare room or kitchen, the principle still applies. So, when attempting to increase one's stock by vegetative means, it should be borne in mind that eventual success owes much to the quality of the parent plant from which leaves or cuttings are taken.

Cuttings with very soft top growth (for example, early spring growth of ivies) should be discarded as they seldom grow well. When started from firm cuttings with two leaves on the stem, and cut about half an inch below the lower leaf joint, the ivies, vines (*Rhoicissus rhomboidea* and *Cissus antarctica*) and smaller-leaved philodendrons are among the easiest

A polythene bag can be used as a home-made propagator. A loop of wire inside the bag will keep the moist polythene from touching the leaves of the cutting and causing them to rot

houseplants to propagate. The majority of these plants will also be better, in the long run, if they have their growing tips removed once they have become established as this will encourage the growth of side shoots.

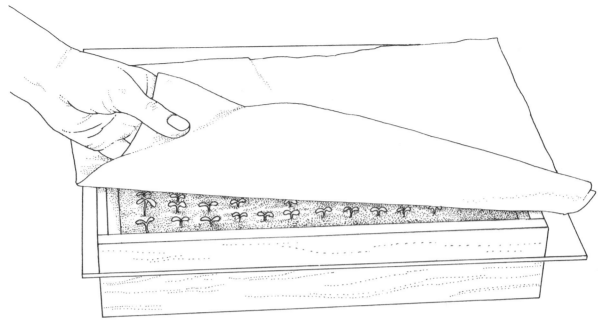

A warm dark environment is required for germinating seeds. This can easily be created by using a pane of glass and an old newspaper

Seed sowing

Seed sowing is relatively simple and, if instructions are provided on the seed packet, they should be followed. Make sure that the pots to be used and the soil mixture are clean. Also moisten the soil mixture before sowing the seed. On the whole, seeds of houseplants should be sown thinly and lightly covered before damping the soil surface with tepid water applied with a watering-can fitted with a fine rose. Germination time will be reduced if a sheet of glass is placed on top of the pot; there should be about half an inch between the soil surface and the glass, and to avoid excessive condensation the glass should be turned daily. It is also helpful if the glass is covered with a sheet of newspaper until such time as germination occurs. The paper can be dispensed with when growth appears, and, at the same time, it will also be beneficial if a wedge is placed between the glass and the pot to permit the entry of a little fresh air. Seedlings should not be exposed to strong sunlight, and a temperature in the region of 18°C (65°F) is preferred.

It is common knowledge that the majority of flowering pot plants are raised from seed in their millions each year; for example calceolarias, cinerarias and primulas. For practical purposes, however, it would be unwise to purchase packets of seed in order to grow a few plants on the window-sill. Where a few

plants only are required it is very much better to purchase young plants ready for potting up, or buy established plants in small pots and to pot them on into slightly larger containers as soon as purchased. Having too many plants to handle properly, which could result if one sowed one's own seed, almost inevitably results in them all becoming congested and few doing as well as they might.

The layman is frequently surprised to learn that many of our bolder plants are, in fact, grown from seed, and not from cuttings as might be expected. Among them are monstera, _Grevillea robusta_, _Fatsia japonica_, _Schefflera actinophylla_ and _Dizygotheca elegantissima_, which is really more graceful than bold in its early stages of development.

Comparatively easy to propagate from leaf cuttings, the African violet (saintpaulia) may also be increased by means of seed. Here again it is important that seedlings be spaced out as soon as this becomes necessary, and only sufficient to meet one's need should be kept – with just a few extras for special friends! Saintpaulias and other plants with very fine seeds should be thinly sown on the surface of moist compost and left uncovered, except for the glass top cover. To encourage growth, saintpaulia compost should be moistened with warm water before sowing; and, when germination takes place, growth will be more active if the seedlings have the benefit of artificial light for a few hours in the evening.

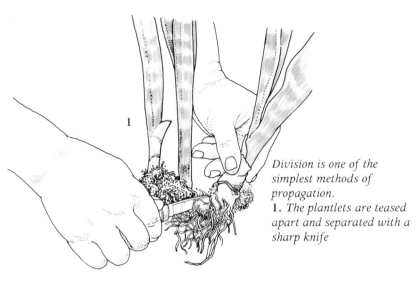

Division is one of the simplest methods of propagation.
1. The plantlets are teased apart and separated with a sharp knife

2. Ensure that each portion has plenty of roots and then pot individually in the usual way

Division

Division of pot plants is a simple operation that is similar to separating a clump of garden plants of the Michaelmas daisy type. Generally speaking, as with propagation of most indoor plants, it is a task that ought to be performed in the spring when the plants are becoming active again. Before separating root clumps the compost should be thoroughly saturated so that the roots can be more easily pulled apart. If it is necessary, use a sharp knife to cut through roots that have become matted together. Complete the operation by potting the separated clumps into individual pots in the usual manner, using John Innes No. 2 potting compost or a soilless potting compost and 3½-in pots.

The following are some of the plants that may be increased by means of division: *Acorus gramineus, Aspidistra lurida, Isolepis gracilis.*

Air layering

For this, one should have to hand the following items: a sharp knife, a 2 ft cane, two handfuls of wet sphagnum moss, a piece of polythene about 8 in by 6 in (a stout polythene bag slit down the side and along the bottom is suitable), string, a piece of matchstick and some one to assist with the operation. Begin by removing a leaf at the height you wish your plant to be. Follow this by getting your helper to hold the stem in position while you cut halfway through the main stem about 1 in below the joint from which the leaf was removed. Then bend the stem carefully, and very slightly so that the knife can be turned to make an upward cut through the actual node. (The flow of latex will do no harm, though care should be taken not to get it on one's clothing,

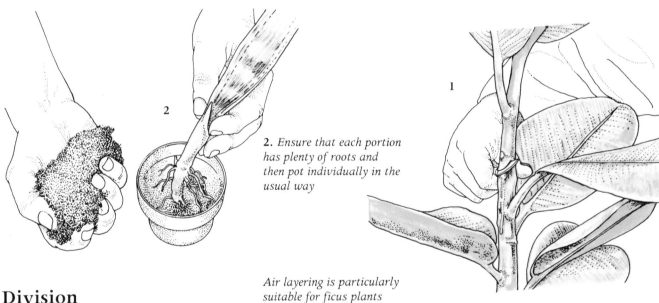

Air layering is particularly suitable for ficus plants (rubber plants) that have lost their lower leaves
1. Make a cut into the stem

2. Insert a matchstick to keep the cut open

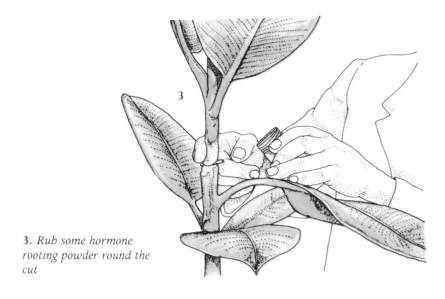

3. *Rub some hormone rooting powder round the cut*

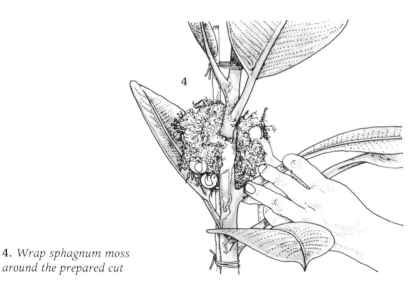

4. *Wrap sphagnum moss around the prepared cut*

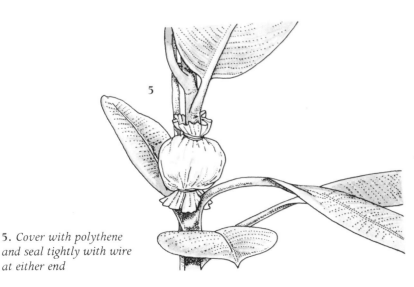

5. *Cover with polythene and seal tightly with wire at either end*

as such stains are difficult to remove). Insert the piece of matchstick in the cut to hold it open, then dust with one of the hormone rooting powders. The cane should now be tied in position above and below the cut mark in the form of a splint and inserted in the pot. This will obviate the possibility of the stem keeling over and breaking off.

The wet moss is then placed on either side of the cut mark and tied in position. Wrap the moss around with the polythene and tie it tightly above and below the moss. After some six to eight weeks, when a plentiful supply of white roots can be seen inside the polythene, use secateurs to sever the rooted section just below the moss ball. Allow the severed end to dry, and carefully remove the polythene before potting the plant into a peaty compost, with the moss ball intact. The compost is watered in to settle it down and is then kept on the dry side until the plant is obviously seen to be growing away in the mixture, when normal watering can begin.

The remaining lower portion of the plant will then produce shoots from the topmost leaf joints, but in the process, it is usual for the plant to shed some of its lower leaves.

Layering

Several houseplants can be increased by this method, which is probably the most reliable of all as the parent plant continues to nourish young plantlets while they are producing roots of their own. One of the best-known examples of this method of propagation is the production of new strawberry plants from strawberry runners.

Common indoor plants that can be produced in this way are chlorophytum, *Saxifraga sarmentosa* and *Tolmiea menziesii*. The operation is simply performed by pegging down the young plantlets into small pots of compost, using a hairpin, or similar piece of bent wire. John Innes No. 1 potting compost with a little extra sharp sand added, is a suitable growing medium or a soilless compost including silver sand. When young plants are obviously growing away on their own roots, the stalks attaching them to the parent plant can be severed.

Other plants that can be increased in much the same way are the hederas, *Ficus pumila*, *F. radicans*, columneas, *Gynura sarmentosa* and the smaller-leaved philodendrons. For these, rather than peg growths down into individual pots, I find it better to place the parent plant in the centre of a shallow box that contains a 3-in layer of John Innes No. 1

potting compost or a soilless equivalent. Longer growths from the plant can then be pegged down in the compost. When rooted, they can be snipped away from the parent and potted up into individual pots using a similar compost. The leaves in the area of the roots should be removed, to prevent them rotting and causing disease. At least three rooted strands should be put into a 3½-in pot, to form an attractive display.

Leaf cuttings

For successful results with this method of propagation, especial care should be taken to provide ideal growing conditions. These include a humid atmosphere and a temperature of 16–18°C (60–65°F). A small propagating case is the easiest way of providing these conditions, but it is not essential. Choice of suitable propagating material is doubly important here, so the use of firm, unblemished leaves is particularly important.

The best-known houseplant propagated by leaf cuttings is the saintpaulia, which roots with little difficulty either in a proper compost, or when the leaf stalk is placed in water. For the latter method a narrow-necked bottle should be used, so that the petiole (leaf stalk) is in the water and the leaf is supported by the neck of the bottle. *Peperomia caperata* and *P. hederaefolia* can also be increased by this method.

If the leaves are to be rooted in compost, rather than water, the severed ends of the leaf stalks can be treated with a hormone rooting powder before inserting them. An open sandy compost should be used into which the leaf stalks can be gently pushed without bruising them. They should not be inserted too deeply, just far enough for them to remain erect. In reasonable conditions, new growth will be apparent about six weeks after insertion of the cuttings.

As mentioned elsewhere, it is a simple matter to propagate streptocarpus from firm, and mature leaves which have been cut into about 4 in lengths. These sections are put into

Chlorophytum plantlets pegged down into small pots will soon form roots and grow away into new plants

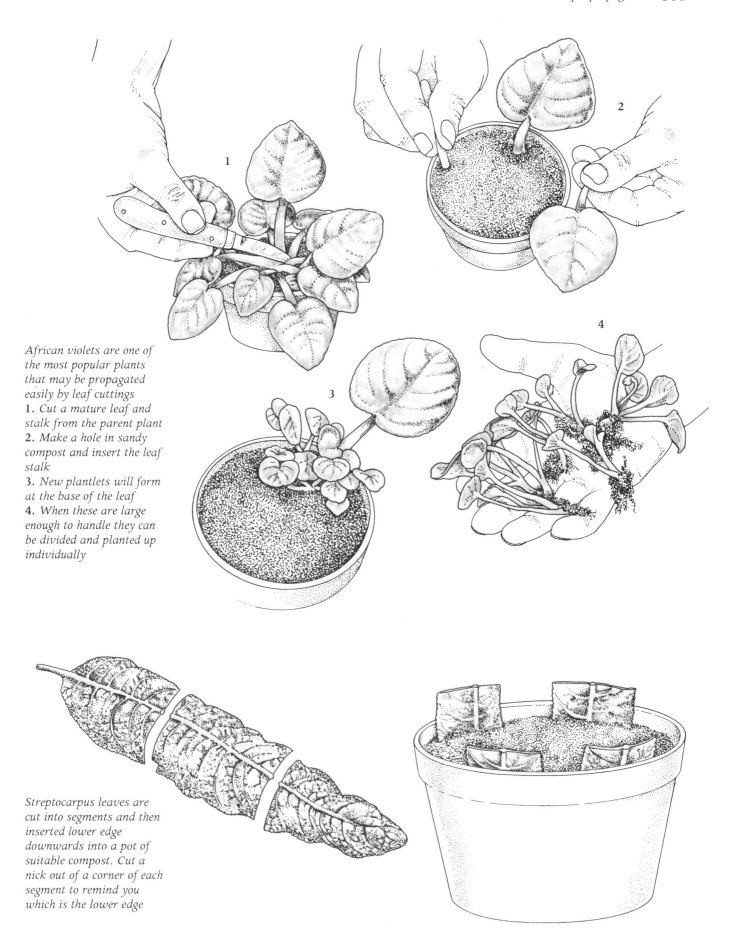

African violets are one of the most popular plants that may be propagated easily by leaf cuttings
1. Cut a mature leaf and stalk from the parent plant
2. Make a hole in sandy compost and insert the leaf stalk
3. New plantlets will form at the base of the leaf
4. When these are large enough to handle they can be divided and planted up individually

Streptocarpus leaves are cut into segments and then inserted lower edge downwards into a pot of suitable compost. Cut a nick out of a corner of each segment to remind you which is the lower edge

the compost; care must be taken that the sections are put in the right way up that is, with the portion of the leaf which was nearest the stem downwards. It helps if a small piece is removed from the bottom corner of each leaf piece.

Stand each piece upright in a mixture of peat and sand, provide the necessary warm, moist conditions and rooting soon takes place.

The Christmas and Easter cactus (Zygocactus and Schlumbergera) are among the easiest of plants to increase from leaves. Segments are removed in the summer when the plants are not in flower, and placed around the outer edge of a small pot filled with peaty potting mixture. Water in lightly, then keep moist and warm.

Another type of propagation in which leaves are used is one in which the leaves are cut up into pieces. This method is particularly suitable for begonias of the rex type. Again, choice of material is important, and crisp leaves of medium size should be selected.

Christmas cactus plants are easily propagated from leaf cuttings. Segments are removed when the plant is not in flower and placed round the edge of a pot filled with peaty compost

These are cut up into small pieces a little larger than a postage stamp, then placed on moist peat with the coloured side uppermost. It is important that the compost should only be moist; if it is too wet the cuttings will rot, while if it is too dry they will shrivel up. As a rough guide, the soil is sufficiently moist if one can just squeeze moisture from the peat, or compost, when a fistful is tightly compressed. Cover the pot with a small piece of glass (turn it daily) and keep the temperature at around 18°C (65°F). Direct sunlight on the cuttings will be damaging, but a light position must be provided, and additional artificial light in the evening is an advantage. About six weeks will elapse before the first tiny leaves appear.

Offsets

Many plants form perfectly shaped miniature replicas of themselves around the stem base of the parent plant, and when reasonably mature these can be very easily cut away with a sharp knife and potted up individually in small pots. The bromeliads respond especially well to this method of propagation. Although not all of them produce offsets at their base, those that do (*Aechmea rhodocyanea* and *Neoregelia carolinae tricolor* in particular) offer what must be one of the most reliable means of propagation of almost all indoor plants. At all stages of growth, from propagation onwards, the bromeliads should have a peaty and free draining potting mixture in which to grow.

Other methods

At the beginning of this chapter, mention was made of the fact that nurserymen rarely resort to other than traditional methods in order to increase their stock. However, there is no reason why the amateur should not display in his collection a wide variety of interesting plants that have been raised from date stones, pineapple tops and the like.

Pips and stones

Given a temperature of 18°C (65°F), oranges, grapefruit, lemons, lychees, avocado pears and a host of other interesting plants can be raised indoors from pips or stones. Growing these is one thing, getting them to produce a crop of fruit is quite a different matter. Although plants will occasionally and quite inexplicably bear fruit when little more than 18 months old, it is more likely that eight to ten years will elapse before any fruit develops, by which time the plant will be more suited to the spacious greenhouse or conservatory, having outgrown its welcome indoors. Though a source of keen interest, it is unfortunate that many of the plants that can be grown from pips and stones of tropical fruits do not in fact develop into plants that are attractive or even suitable for indoor decoration; this seldom deters an interested person.

Should you have a mind to experiment, it is important to follow the advice given in this chapter for the sowing of seed, and to pot the resultant plants on into standard houseplant potting mixture as the seedlings increase in size. Also, it is important to allow the seed of citrus plants, avocado pears and dates to dry off before they are sown.

Avocado pear stones
One of the more attractive plants to grow from a stone is the avocado. The very large stone is best started into growth in water, although it will also germinate in soil, but this takes longer. The stone should be suspended to about half its depth in water. This can be done by inserting three cocktail sticks around the circumference of the stone and placing it in a glass of water so that the sticks rest on the rim of the glass. Roots will sprout in the water, and when the stone splits to produce leaves the stone can be planted in peaty soil with the leafy top section exposed. The plant can then be grown on in a moderate temperature in a cool room. Bushy growth can be achieved by pinching out the growing tips regularly.

Pineapple tops
Propagating pineapples in the home is not easy, but, if successful, it does give one that bit of an edge over one's friends who are also indoor plant enthusiasts. When attempting this, several methods may be employed, but I have seen the following succeed, which is some recommendation. A pineapple with a healthy green top should be selected and the top should be removed with a sharp knife, leaving just a sliver of the fruit still attached. A 5-in pot is filled with bromeliad potting mixture (see page 56), and a thin layer of sharp sand scattered over the surface. The pineapple top is then placed on the sand, and pushed gently into the compost, which should be kept moist. A temperature of at least 18°C (65°F) should be maintained. Roots will form more readily in the sand, and having done so will then find their way into the compost underneath. Once rooted, culture is the same as that advised for other bromeliads (see pages 52–56).

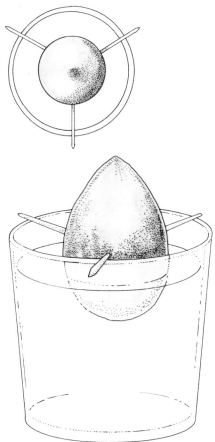

Avocado stones are best started into growth in water. Insert three cocktail sticks into the stone as shown above and rest them on the rim of a glass of water so that the stone is half submerged

Some common problems

Over the past thirty years houseplants have advanced from very humble beginnings to the point where they have become one of the most popular hobbies, competing strongly with such well-established pastimes as fishing and outdoor gardening. Unfortunately the more plants there are the more problems arise and the more one is beset by questions.

I find that whatever the company, if it leaks out that I am involved with houseplants, there is an inevitable flood of questions from all and sundry enquiring about their rubber plant, African violet or dumb cane. Taking part in a regular monthly 'Phone-In' programme I have learnt that the subject of houseplants runs second only to pets in the numbers of questions asked. Being a sort of Aunt Agatha for one of the world's largest producers of houseplants, I am also obliged to cope with a vast number of written questions, as well as dealing with the endless queries and problems following talks on houseplants. Flower shows, such as Chelsea are another time for answering questions when floods of visitors ask about every conceivable sort of plant.

This chapter is devoted to some of the questions that I am most frequently asked together with a few which are less common but interesting nevertheless.

Green poinsettia

Q I have kept my poinsettia plant in beautiful condition from last year, but the red bracts that were on the plant when it came will not form. Is it possible to get them to develop again?

A Modern poinsettias are, in fact, very much easier to care for and to keep from year to year than they used to be. In order to get bracts in subsequent years, plants must not be exposed to artificial light from the end of September through until Christmas. They are what is termed short-day plants. This means they flower naturally during the shorter winter days of the year, therefore it is essential to ensure that during this period they are not exposed to any artificial light in the evening. It is, however, important to ensure that plants have the lightest possible location during the hours of natural daylight.

The shrimp plant

Q Having flowered for most of the summer, the bracts of my shrimp plant are now beginning to fall off, and some of the leaves are changing colour to a reddish-brown. What is the cause, and can cuttings be taken from my plant?

A It is usual for the shrimp plant, *Beloperone guttata*, to stop producing its colourful bracts in the autumn, and for existing bracts to lose much of their colour. When these are no longer attractive they should be removed. Plants may also be pruned to shape in the autumn; firm trimmings, a few inches in length, will root readily in any good potting mixture. When growing conditions are cold and wet, the leaves have a tendency to change colour and may in some instances drop off, but, unless this loss of leaves is excessive, it should not give rise to concern. After the plants have flowered, the compost must be kept on the dry side until the following spring when normal watering can be resumed. A winter temperature in the region of 55°F (13°C) should be maintained, and the parent plant can be potted on into a larger pot in early spring.

Sansevieria in flower

Q My sansevieria plant, which I have cherished for the past four years, is now in flower; is this unusual?

A It is unusual for smaller plants to do so, but older plants flower in mid-summer with reasonable regularity, though there is no way of ensuring this.

Ungainly aphelandra

Q I have an *Aphelandra squarrosa* plant that has lost its lower leaves, but has two strong healthy shoots at the top. Is there anything I can do to improve the appearance of my plant?

A Although little can be done to improve the appearance of your plant, there is no reason why the two healthy shoots should not be removed and used to propagate two new plants. Do this by allowing the shoots to produce two pairs of firm leaves before severing them with a sharp knife from the parent plant and inserting them in 3-in pots filled with John Innes No. 1 potting compost. To prevent the cutting from drying out, place both pot and cutting in a sealed polythene bag and protect the latter from strong sunlight; the temperature should be in the region of 65°F (18°C). Cuttings should be started in individual pots, and as soon as they have rooted through to the sides of these they must be potted on into 5-in pots using John Innes No. 2 potting compost. After removal of the growth from which the cuttings are made, the parent plant will be of little further use and should be disposed of.

Wilted cyclamen

Q Is there anything one can do to revive cyclamen plants that have wilted as a result of becoming too dry?

A Simply giving the plant water will not result in the flowers becoming erect again, although the leaves will stiffen and take on their natural shape. Florists, who are frequently faced with this problem, adopt the practice of watering the plant well before wrapping it fairly tightly in newspaper. This results in the flowers standing erect while they draw up water, and remaining so when the paper is removed.

Bud drop

Q I have an hibiscus that is quite healthy but sheds its flower buds before they open, and a Christmas Cactus that behaves in the same way. Why does this happen?

A Insufficient light is the short answer. Both these plants need a light location to flower well, and will benefit from being placed out of doors in a sunny, sheltered position during the summer months. The Christmas cactus is also very sensitive when it is about to flower. If this plant is moved from its normal growing position by a light window it will tend to shed buds before they have opened; so if they are about to flower the best thing is to leave them alone to get on with it.

Dividing saintpaulias

Q For some years I have been growing an African violet (saintpaulia) which has now developed into a large, bushy plant. What I would like to know is if it can be split up in order to make more plants, and if so, when would be the correct time?

A Yes, this can be done, but you would probably get better results by propagating plants from individual leaves, as described in the chapter, Simple propagation. The plant can be divided up into smaller pieces at almost any time when it is not in flower, though the best time is probably April to May when the divided pieces will root more readily into fresh compost. The plant must be well watered before removing it from its pot. Follow depotting by gently teasing the matted roots apart and pot the separated pieces into small pots filled with a peaty compost. After potting, water the soil with tepid water and then keep the young plants on the dry side until new growth is evident. Normal watering can then begin.

Flowerless saintpaulias

Q I have some beautiful African violet plants that get bigger and bigger, but never produce any flowers. How can I get them to bloom?

A This has become a very popular question in recent years, as better heating has improved growing conditions for saintpaulias indoors. We hear so many reasons for the reluctance of plants to flower, but my view is that there are two very simple answers. One is poor light; it is of the utmost importance that saintpaulias should have very good light if they are to flower. This will usually mean placing the plant by a sunny window during the day and under a table lamp in the evening. This treatment will almost certainly give markedly better results. The second suggestion is that one should try feeding with a fertiliser that contains a higher proportion of potash such as a tomato fertiliser. The usual high-nitrogen houseplant fertilisers are fine for producing bigger foliage plants but will not encourage production of flowers.

Naughty pussy

Q My cat has done its business in the Swiss cheese plant. This was actually asked, to my horror, on a live radio programme one morning!

A The lady questioner in fact wanted to know why the cat should have done such a thing and what she could do about it. My answer was that she should not invite the neighbours in for a few days! On a more serious note I told her to remove the 'business' with as much of the surrounding compost as possible. The resultant hole should then be filled with fresh compost, and a lid made for the pot to prevent any repetition. (I never cease to be amazed by the odd problems that confront many growers of indoor plants.)

Ailing fatsias

Q My *Fatsia japonica* plant, given to me some months ago, is now looking very sad and is reduced to two large and one small leaf at the top of the stem. Can anything be done to restore it to its former appearance?

A Alas, when growing in the home, very little can be done to revive house plants when they have been reduced to the condition you describe. There is no reason, however, why you should not plant your *F. japonica* out in the garden in a sheltered position. For best results, summer planting is advised. In time the fatsia will develop into a very fine garden shrub, which seems to thrive even in smoke-polluted districts.

The rubber plant's sheath

Q Should I remove the pink-coloured covering from around the new leaf of my Rubber plant in order to help it open?

A Certainly not! The sheath is Mother Nature's way of protecting the young leaf and should be allowed to fall off naturally when it has completed its protective function. Many ficus leaves are irreparably damaged by removing the sheath prematurely; also by inquisitive fingers handling the sheath before it has opened.

One big leaf

Q My Rubber plant, purchased recently, has one leaf turning yellow – what is the cause? It is the bottom leaf of the plant, and is much larger than the others.

A This means simply that the leaf you mention is the one that was attached to the parent piece of stem when the plant was propagated as a cutting, and having completed its function it is quite natural for it to turn yellow and eventually die. Many nurserymen remove this leaf before dispatching plants, using a sharp knife to carefully cut it off below soil level.

Problems with flowers

Q My flowering pot plants always look lovely when I take them home, but the flowers soon die and some of the buds fall off before they even open. What is going wrong?

A Usually poor light is to blame once again. It is essential that all flowering plants in the home should have good light in which to grow if flowers and buds are to function correctly. In good light flowers will have a brighter colour and remain attractive for much longer than if they are in poor light. Hibiscus, in particular, find life difficult in poor light, and will usually shed their flower buds before they open.

When placed by a window most plants will need some protection from very bright sunlight, but it is most important not to place them in poorly lit corners if you wish to get the best from them.

Brown spots

Q Lots of my plants have developed irregular brown marks and spots for no apparent reason but the condition doesn't seem to spread. What's the problem?

A There are numerous possibilities, but the most common reason for damage of this kind is the use of aerosol sprays near to where the plant has been standing. Examples of guilty products are furniture polish, hair lacquers and fly sprays. On plant foliage you should only use sprays and insecticides that are specifically intended for them. All other sprays should be kept well away or the plants themselves moved to a safe place when you are polishing.

Damage may also result through using leaf-cleaner sprays intended for plants either too generously or too frequently, while plants are standing in the sun or when the temperature is very low.

Limp leaves

Q My African violet plants have become mottled around the edge of the leaves, which have also become rather limp to the touch. Why is this so?

A Almost without question this is due to low temperatures, and is usually more common during the winter months. To do well saintpaulias should have a minimum temperature of not less than 18°C (65°F). They will survive at lower temperatures, but to grow well they must be warm. Quite often damage of this kind can occur in a cold shop before the purchase is made, or as a result of carrying plants home on cold days with insufficient wrapping. When buying plants it is worth inspecting the leaves to see that they are firm and free from blemishes.

Treatment of Ficus benjamina

Q During the summer I potted my 3½-ft-tall plant of *Ficus benjamina* into a 9-in pot, using John Innes No. 3 Potting Compost. Two months after potting I started giving the plant regular applications of liquid fertiliser, a little each time the plant was watered. Many of the leaves are now turning yellow and the plant appears to be sick; I am wondering what could have gone wrong?

A Almost everything! First, a 9-in pot is much too large for a ficus plant that is only $3\frac{1}{2}$-ft in height, and the John Innes Compost used would have been better for the addition of a little extra peat or leaf-mould in the mixture. Also, plants potted indoors in mid-summer should not need any form of fertiliser until the following spring at the earliest; unnecessary feeding damages young roots, the consequence of which is yellow leaves. It would be better now if the plant was kept on the dry side in a warm room until it shows signs of recovery.

Variegated ivies and tradescantias turning green

Q Why, after a few months, do my variegated ivies and tradescantias turn green in colour?

A The reason for this is almost invariably lack of light. Plants purchased in the summer months retain their colouring while growing in a light window, but quickly revert to green in the winter if maximum light is not provided. It is odd, however, that cuttings taken from the green growth of ivy plants will frequently sprout with variegated colouring. Tradescantias, besides being kept in a light position should have any green growth removed as it appears, as it is much more vigorous and will quickly predominate.

Leggy Ivy

Q My hedera has become very thin and leggy. Is there anything that can be done to improve its appearance.

A The best treatment really is to plant the ivy out in the garden, preferably against a wall where it can climb naturally. The larger-leaved ivies, such as *H. canariensis*, make superb climbing plants, while the smaller-leaved ones are excellent ground cover subjects. Indoors ivies require cool and light conditions to give of their best.

Red spider mite on ivy

Q Why has my *Hedera canariensis* plant taken on a dry appearance with browning of the leaf margins?

A The short answer is red spider mite. These minute pests thrive in very dry and warm conditions, and have a particular liking for for the *canariensis* ivy. These pests can be detected by the naked eye if one knows what one is looking for, but it usually requires a magnifying glass to see their tiny bodies moving around. Where there are very bad infestations these mites will produce tiny webs between the leaf and leaf stalk. Erradicating red spider mite is not easy, but perseverance will usually bring its reward. A suitable insecticide should be mixed according to the manufacturer's directions then applied to both the upper and lower surfaces of the leaves, ensuring that the plant is completely saturated. Whenever one is treating plants with insecticide rubber gloves should be worn and the job should be done out of doors or in a shed. Choose a still warm day if the job is to be done outside and keep treated plants out of the sun.

Red spider mites dislike moist cool conditions, so it is a good idea to mist the foliage over regularly with a fine spray of water as a deterrent. Inspect all your plants periodically for signs of infestation as prevention is much better than cure.

Decreasing monstera

Q The leaves of my monstera plant seem to be getting smaller and they don't have the usual cut marks in them. Why is this happening?

A Poor culture is the main problem usually allied to less than adequate light conditions. Poor culture can mean a number of things. The drainage may be poor or the temperature may be too low – if it falls below 16°C (60°F) too often the plant will begin to suffer. The plant may be in need of potting into fresh compost or feeding. Any of these factors in combination with cold, dark and wet conditions make the worst environment for any plant and it is not surprising that its appearance begins to deteriorate.

Roots of a Swiss cheese plant

Q What can I do with the long things hanging down from my Swiss cheese plant?

A These are aerial roots and a natural part of the plant. In the wild they spread out over the forest floor and into water holes seeking moisture and nutrients for the plant. Removal of some of these will not be harmful, but it is unwise to take them all off. The best method of keeping them under control is to tie the roots loosely in around the stem and when they are long enough, poke them into the potting compost. An interesting exercise can be conducted whereby the roots are directed into a container of water standing adjacent to the pot. They will then draw up moisture from this source and the soil the plant grows in need not be watered so frequently.

Brown marks on foliage

Q Some of my plants are getting funny brown marks on them but I cannot find any sign of pests. What could be the cause?

A I am asked this question so often at flower shows or in letters through the post accompanied by samples of the damaged leaves. Almost invariably, dry brown blotches, more particularly streaks, on otherwise healthy leaves are the result of placing plants too close to window panes on very sunny days; this can be especially harmful if the glass has a frosted pattern. The window pane acts as a magnifying glass, increasing the intensity of the sun's rays which literally burn the surface of the leaf. Even old rubber plants that one might think would resist any such damage are vulnerable.

Plants for a dark room

Q What sort of plant can you recommend for a dark room that is not very well heated?

A There really is very little that one can suggest with confidence, as reasonable light is essential for almost all indoor plants, and, if they are to have any chance of producing new leaves the temperature should be maintained at around 16°C (60°F). Some will tolerate less, but this is a minimum for most plants. Darker locations are really only suitable for the tougher green foliage plants such as the aspidistra, rhoicissus and *Philodendron scandens*.

House plants and central heating

Q I recently moved into a new house with large windows and central heating that maintains a minimum temperature of 65°F (18°C). Could you please suggest a small collection of plants that would be suitable for a beginner in these conditions?

A Ideally, you should choose plants that are both easy to grow and able to withstand the conditions prevailing in the temperature you mention. Some of the easier plants, ivies and *Cissus antarctica* for example, do not grow particularly well at higher temperatures. A selection from the following plants will give you a good mixture that will be reasonably easy to care for; *Maranta leuconeura kerchoveana, M. l. erythrophylla,* monstera, *Philodendron scandens, Rhoicissus rhomboidea,* peperomias, pileas, *Hypocyrta glabra, Anthurium scherzerianum* and *Sansevieria trifasciata*

laurentii. It is wise to experiment with a small collection of this kind, getting to know the individual requirements of particular plants, before attempting more difficult sorts.

Effects of gas and paraffin heaters

Q Are gas and paraffin fumes harmful to plants?

A Yes, fumes of either polluting the atmosphere would almost inevitably result in plants shedding leaves and in flowers failing to survive. In this respect both tomato plants and cut flowers of carnation are especially sensitive, and could well be used as vectors for harmful fumes. However, modern appliances burning natural gas are generally not harmful. Paraffin heaters in sealed rooms that are seldom aired will be detrimental to some plants and fatal to others. Calor gas fires are not by any means suitable for all plants, and should be the suspected culprit if topmost, or young leaves show signs of distress.

The benefits of cold tea

Q Is cold tea good for plants?

A If my experience of listening to growers of houseplants extolling the virtues of cold tea is anything to go by, then I would most heartily approve of this liquid that is often treated with a certain amount of amusement. The benefit lies in the fact that the water has been boiled so all the impurities have been removed and cold tea is almost the perfect example of tepid water; whether or not the tea itself has any nutritional value is a different matter.

Fertilisers for houseplants

Q With so many different fertilisers being offered for sale I find difficulty in choosing the right one for my indoor plants. Could you please advise? Also, could you give me some advice on how often and when I should feed my plants?

A The formula for indoor plant fertilisers varies very little and there is no reason why they should not all give equally good results if used according to the maker's directions. Some of the more vigorous plants, such as aphelandra, will benefit, however, if fertilisers are applied at shorter intervals, or slightly in excess of the recommended strength. As to their use, the principal precaution here is to ensure that the soil in the pot is moist before applying the fertiliser, otherwise root damage may result. They should be used mainly in spring and summer when the plants are producing new leaves, although weak feeding in winter may also be necessary if the plants are actively growing. Feeding plants that are sick and have ceased to grow during the normal growing season will only be detrimental. Such plants should be carefully nursed back to health and fed only when growth is again active.

Potting composts

Q Can you please tell me if ordinary garden soil will be suitable for potting my house plants into? If not, what do you recommend?
A In the first place, there is no such commodity as 'ordinary' garden soil, as soil varies from district to district and even from one garden to the next. Garden soil, unless of particularly high quality, is generally considered to be too heavy and lacking in porosity for the majority of potted plants. For many years now the emphasis, as far as the majority of commercial house plant growers are concerned, has been on an open mixture that contains a high percentage of peat. The success of peat-based soilless composts helps to prove this point. These mixes and the John Innes range of composts can be purchased in handy packs that are clean and labour saving. John Innes compost should have extra peat added to it for the majority of house plants. When purchasing compost it is wise to buy sufficient for one's immediate needs only, as composts tend to dry out and deteriorate when stored for any length of time.

Planting of foliage and flowering plants

Q Could you please tell me how to care for a container of mixed foliage and flowering plants given to me as a Christmas present?
A Most bowls of assorted plants are prepared for festive occasions and contain at least one colourful flowering plant that will probably die a month or two after purchase. When no longer attractive the flowering plant should be removed, and the hole which is left can be filled with fresh compost. As many of these containers have no drainage holes, water should be given sparingly to prevent the compost becoming waterlogged. Although not all plants are compatible, it is surprising how well many will grow when planted together in this fashion.

Plant care at holiday time

Q I own a number of indoor plants and am wondering what I should do with them while on holiday.
A For the summer vacation, it is usually best to get a friend to see to watering for you in your own home during your absence. Plants can be taken to the friend's house, but they seem to resent change once they have adjusted themselves to particular surroundings. It is of the utmost importance that the chosen person should be given precise directions concerning the amount and frequency of watering and fertilising, as the novice is inclined to go to extremes, one way or the other. Failing this, the plants should be removed from sunny windows and given a good watering before grouping them together in a large watertight plant holder, or basin. A 4-in. layer of wet sand in the bottom of the basin will help to keep the compost moist in your absence; packing the pots around with moist peat, moss or wet newspaper will also be an advantage. During the winter months plants will be faced with the additional hazard of low temperatures, which makes it essential that they be moved to premises with similar conditions to those of your own home whilst you are away.

Exhibiting houseplants

Q Our local flower show is including a section for house plants this year for the first time – have you any advice to offer a would-be exhibitor?
A Many flower shows now have a class for house plants, and judges are presented with many problems when assessing the merits of the large number of plants that come under this general heading. Some of them are comparatively easy to care for, while others are downright difficult. Naturally enough, healthy plants will catch the judge's eye, but when faced with plants of equal merit he will look for other points in their favour. So plants should be clean and neat, which will entail the removal of dead and damaged leaves, and the tying-in of untidy growth on plants such as ivies and philodendrons. Even pots should have their share of titivating, as clean pots set off plants to much better advantage. The naming of plants will also be a consideration, so ensure that the names, and the way these are spelt, are correct.

INDEX

Metrication table

Imperial	Metric
$\frac{1}{2}$ in	1 cm
1 in	2.5 cm
$1\frac{1}{2}$ in	4 cm
2 in	5 cm
3 in	8 cm
4 in	10 cm
5 in	13 cm
6 in	15 cm
7 in	18 cm
8 in	20 cm
9 in	23 cm
10 in	25 cm
11 in	28 cm
1 foot	30 cm
2 ft	60 cm
3 ft	1 m